THE HISTORIC
RESTAURANTS OF PARIS

✦

THE HISTORIC
RESTAURANTS OF PARIS

ELLEN WILLIAMS

THE LITTLE BOOKROOM · NEW YORK

COPYRIGHT

© BY
ELLEN
WILLIAMS
Design by

Louise Fili Ltd. Cover: Jean Béraud, *La Pâtisserie Gloppe* (1889), Musée de la Ville de Paris, Musée Carnavalet, Paris, Giraudon/Art Resource, NY. Library of Congress Cataloging-in-Publication Data.

Williams, Ellen. Historic
Restaurants of Paris/by
Ellen Williams. p. cm.
Includes index.
ISBN 1-892145-03-0
(pbk.) 1. Restaurants
France—   Paris—
Guide-   books 2.
Restau-   rants—
France—   Paris—
History.   I. Title.
TX9075.F   72 P3795
2001 647.   95443'61–
dc21 00-045317 ISBN 1-892145-03-0
Fourth printing, March 2002. All rights
reserved, which includes the right to
reproduce this book or portions there-
of including photographs, in any form
whatsoever, without written permission
of the publisher. Printed in Hong Kong. The
Little Book-   book-room@rcn.com   room, Five St.
Luke's Place   e-mail   NY, NY 10014
t·212 691 3521   f·212 691 2011

Contents

Introduction

PARIS ABOUNDS IN RESTAURANTS AND GOUR-
MET SHOPS THAT HAVE BEEN IN BUSINESS
for more than a hundred years, surviving all the
social, political, and economic upheavals of the
entire turbulent twentieth century. From tiny
boulangeries and *bistros* barely known outside their
own quarters to world-famous cafés and restaurants,
these are businesses that have flourished in a city
where the fiercest culinary competition has ensured
the most rigorous standards. Some are almost completely unchanged since they opened, providing an
entrée into that bygone world of gaslights and
horse-drawn carriages. Some are enterprises that
originated in the nineteenth century but underwent
renovations that obscure their real history. Others
are venerable French institutions now conducting
business in completely modern settings. A few, con-
versely, are new establishments that have taken up
residence in former *épiceries*, *boulangeries*, and
pâtisseries whose preserved decor alone merits
inclusion in these pages.

Among the listings are the most refined temples
of gastronomy as well as working-class *bouillons*,

elegant tea salons and rustic wine bars, cozy *bistros* and bustling *brasseries*. The majority date from the late nineteenth century, the golden age of French cuisine, although several were already fixtures by the time of the French Revolution. The few that were founded in the first years of the twentieth century remain very much products of the glorious era that lasted until the First World War wrenched Belle Epoque Paris into the modern age. Their longevity has depended not only on the quality of the fare they have provided to generations of the world's most discerning customers, but also on the French dedication to a culinary heritage that values the old and trusted above the newfangled or newly fashionable.

In what other city would so many businesses devoted to eating and drinking be protected as historic national monuments? These establishments do more than simply provide sustenance to contemporary diners. In fact, at some of these historic restaurants, the food itself is no longer of great appeal, and yet crowds continue to come year after year, decade after decade, drawn, more than anything, by the romance of the past. Whether still flourishing or merely resting on their laurels, they are a proud part of the national patrimony, providing an unbroken link to a more glorious French past.

This urge to connect with their culinary heritage is not unique to modern-day Parisians. At the 1889 Universal Exposition that celebrated the centennial of the French Revolution, visitors entering an amusement-park reproduction of the Bastille could dine at recreations of the city's old restaurants where they would be served by waiters outfitted in historic dress.

Marcel Proust famously savored his ability to transport himself to an earlier time with one memory-provoking taste of a *madeleine* he had dipped into his lime-blossom tea. At the establishments listed in this guide, nostalgic epicures of today can summon up Proust's Paris as well as the Paris of Balzac, Sand, Zola, and the Impressionists. By visiting the places where those great painters and novelists once shopped and dined, we experience the otherwise lost world of old Paris they so evocatively portrayed.

ELLEN WILLIAMS

ARRONDISSEMENT

✦

Angélina

226, RUE DE RIVOLI (1ST ARR.)
01.42.60.82.00
MÉTRO: TUILERIES
9AM-7PM; CLOSED TUESDAY

✦

MARCEL PROUST, WHO WAS TRANSPORTED BACK TO CHILDHOOD WITH THE TASTE OF the tea cake known as a *madeleine*, was among the early regular customers at this chic *salon de thé* that faces the Tuileries Gardens. Upper-class Parisians like Proust had been drinking tea since the eighteenth century, but it wasn't until the arrival of tea parlors such as Angélina that it was taken up by the *bourgeoisie*.

Founded as Rumpelmeyer by an Austrian pastry chef just three years into the twentieth century, Angélina, with its elaborate gilt moldings, idyllic landscape murals, high-backed, black-leather chairs, and small, marble-topped tables, has always been every bit as elegant as the luxurious Hôtel Meurice, in whose rue de Rivoli arcade it is located. Then as now, it was the province of women, tea salons being one of the few public places where a proper lady could dine unescorted by a man. In fact, as late as World War I, it was illegal for a woman sitting alone to be served at a boulevard café terrace. Left Bank residents Gertrude Stein and Alice B. Toklas regularly traveled across the city to this stylish Right Bank address.

The staff at Angélina is also predominantly female—waitresses in white aprons bustling to deliver light lunches and rich pastries to the patrons, who are often accompanied by children eagerly anticipating their treats. Despite its location in the heart of tourist Paris, locals continue to come, especially for *le chocolat Africain*, generally deemed the best hot chocolate in a city with plenty of worthy competition. Sandwiches, *salades composées* (the *Thiel* contains chicken, ham, *gruyère*, and *haricots verts*) and hot dishes such as seafood curry over basmati rice are typical of the luncheon fare. The pastries include the traditional offerings, the house specialty being the *Mont Blanc*, truly a mountain of meringue, whipped cream, and chestnut cream. A glass case displays the take-away options: cakes, candies, sugared mints, delicately shaped marzipan figures, and packets of *l'Africain* to make at home.

Café Verlet

256, RUE SAINT-HONORÉ (1ST ARR.)
01.42.60.67.39
MÉTRO: PALAIS ROYAL-MUSÉE DU LOUVRE
9AM-7PM; CLOSED SATURDAY & SUNDAY
MAY-OCTOBER, SUNDAY & MONDAY
OCTOBER-MAY; CLOSED AUGUST

✦

"THE BOULEVARDS ARE A LONG CHAIN OF CAFÉS," HENRY JAMES ONCE ASSERTED OF Paris, an observation as true today as it was in the nineteenth century. Far less common, however, are roasters, *brûleries*, devoted to the skilled preparation of the coffee beans that will later be brewed and served in those many cafés. Verlet, in business near the Louvre and the Palais-Royal since 1880, is both—a coffee emporium as well as a café.

Discerning shoppers selecting from more than two dozen freshly roasted varieties displayed in overflowing open burlap sacks are advised by the knowledgeable staff as to the percentage of caffeine each particular blend contains, the altitude at which it was grown, and the key flavor notes an educated palate is meant to appreciate when it is drunk: Guatemalan is fruity with notes of lemon, cloves, and licorice; Indian has notes of humid earth and basmati rice; Kenyan contains notes of black currant, grilled peanuts, and tobacco.

Verlet also stocks more than three dozen fine teas, which are displayed in colorful vintage tole canisters, as well as dried fruits, nuts, and conserves. An espresso, *café crème*, or cappuccino can be taken in the quiet, unadorned wood-paneled shop at one of the small wooden tables. The lunch menu is limited to a small selection of *croque-monsieurs*, *salades composées*, and a choice of rustic pastries that are all made on the premises.

Le Cochon à l'Oreille

15, RUE MONTMARTRE (1ST ARR.)
01.42.36.07.56
MÉTRO: HALLES
7AM-5PM; 8AM-7PM SATURDAY; CLOSED SUNDAY

✦

WHEN ÉMILE ZOLA DUBBED LES HALLES THE "BELLY OF PARIS" IN 1873, HE WAS speaking of a market that had already been active on the Right Bank site for seven centuries. Produce, dairy, sea creatures, chickens, rabbits, and sides of beef were brought here from the French provinces, the farmers arriving after midnight to set up in the covered stalls. Then, from all parts of the city, retailers, restaurateurs, kitchen maids, and housewives would gather together the raw materials for the tables of Paris.

The market lasted here a full century after Zola, until it was finally moved to the suburbs south of the city. A record of the daily cycle of labor the writer described, however, is preserved on the walls of Le Cochon à l'Oreille, one of the neighborhood's oldest surviving working-class *bistros*. Within the beveled-glass entry, the first of three large, *fin-de-siècle* tile murals depicts the market as it once came to life under a pre-dawn sky. In another, we see the

[17]

peak of activity alongside the massive Saint-Eustache (the seventeenth-century church with a chapel dedicated to the market vendors that presides at the head of this very street), with a remarkable variety of wares displayed in wicker baskets and being trundled away by the *forts des Halles*, the brawny porters. Finally, after the closing bell has rung, the wholesale market shuts down just as the rest of Paris begins its day.

Today, most of the patrons of Le Cochon à l'Oreille crowd around the minuscule zinc-topped bar for a quick *café express* or *pastis*. A lucky few seated at one of the four narrow wooden booths select from the small menu: *terrine de maison, oeuf mayonnaise, crudités*, quiche, steak with shallots, *gigot d'agneau, boudin, pied de porc*. Hot meals, however, are available only at lunch.

Note the ancient wood-and-brass telephone just inside the entry, a relic of the days when café owners enthusiastically embraced the new technology as another inducement to bring in paying customers.

L'Escargot-Montorgueil

38, RUE MONTORGUEIL (1ST ARR.)
01.42.36.83.51
MÉTRO: HALLES
12:30PM–2:30PM & 8PM–11PM
CLOSED MONDAY

✦

IN 1878, WHEN CLAUDE MONET WANTED TO PAINT A WORKING-CLASS STREET DECKED out for a national holiday with hundreds of fluttering tricolors, he chose the rue Montorgueil, setting up his easel among the fishmongers who used the street to transport their catch from northern ports into the city's central market at Les Halles. Monet might well have stopped for lunch at L'Escargot-Montorgueil, which was already a landmark on the street, having opened nearly fifty years earlier, specializing, of course, in snails.

Although the quarter has yet to recover from the departure of the wholesale food stalls some thirty years ago, people still come to the area for its legendary restaurants. This one is a particularly picturesque holdover from the early days, and boasts what must be the most varied preparations of *escargots* in Paris: with mint, with *roquefort*, in a casse-

[19]

role, in puff pastry with mushrooms, in a hollowed-out potato, in a *terrine*, with fennel, curried, or simply *à la bourgogne* (with garlic, butter, and parsley). Oysters, another specialty of the house, have been served since around 1890, shortly before the enormous gilded snail and its many offspring were added to the original black-and-gold façade.

Just inside the entrance is a ceiling painting that once graced the dining parlor of the great French *tragedienne* Sarah Bernhardt. A lovely spiral staircase connects the lower- and upper-level dining rooms, which are variously decorated with worn wood paneling, enormous etched mirrors, and small framed prints on walls that have been covered with charming *toile de Jouy* fabric. Diners who don't care for snails can order chilled artichokes, marinated peppers, smoked salmon, beef *carpaccio*, or swordfish in a vinegar sauce, among other choices.

Le Grand Véfour

17, RUE DE BEAUJOLAIS (1ST ARR.)
01.42.96.56.27
MÉTRO: PALAIS ROYAL-MUSÉE DU LOUVRE
12:30PM-2PM & 7:30PM-10:15PM
CLOSED SATURDAY & SUNDAY

✦

STANDING IN THE TRANQUIL CENTER GARDEN OF THE PALAIS-ROYAL, IT SEEMS IMPOSSIBLE that just beyond the enclosing buildings lies one of the busiest sections of the most densely populated capital in Europe. And because this enclave is almost hidden—the entrances inconspicuously tucked into the street-side façades—it is hard to believe that two hundred years ago the Palais-Royal was known as "the capital of Paris." If these arcaded walls could talk, they would tell a tale of the usurers, gaming houses, and brothels that openly conducted business here in the late eighteenth century, when the gardens were the setting of assassinations, duels, and revolutionary plottings. In fact, it was in a Palais-Royal café that Camille Desmoulins rallied the disgruntled populace to arms just before the storming of the Bastille.

One of the most historic establishments within

the gardens is Le Grand Véfour, the oldest restaurant in Paris still operating on its original site. Napoleon and Josephine, Honoré de Balzac, George Sand, and Victor Hugo are among its illustrious former diners, and their names have been engraved on small plaques above the seats they purportedly once occupied.

In the decade before the French Revolution, these premises contained the Café de Chartres, whose name is still emblazoned above the garden-side entrance. In 1820, Jean Véfour purchased and rechristened the restaurant and commissioned the exquisite Pompeian-style paintings on the walls that make this one of the most distinctive and distinguished dining rooms in the world.

Le Grand Véfour's fortunes have risen and fallen over the many decades of its existence. Today, it is once again rated among the stellar restaurants in the city, with a menu that features ravioli stuffed with *foie gras* and black truffles, Osetra caviar served with blinis, *confit* of Bresse chicken, *noisettes d'agneau* dusted in ground coffee beans, turbot with tomatoes and a *mousseline* of almonds. Among the unusual desserts are an artichoke *torte* and a fennel *confit* with a red-pepper *sorbet*. The *chariot à fromages* is one of the highlights of a meal here.

Maison Cador

PÂTISSERIE ST-GERMAIN-L'AUXERROIS

2, RUE DE L'AMIRAL DE COLIGNY (1ST ARR.)
01.45.08.19.18
MÉTRO: LOUVRE-RIVOLI
9AM-7PM; CLOSED MONDAY

✦

ITS LOCATION DIRECTLY FACING THE EASTERN END OF THE LOUVRE MIGHT LEAD YOU TO assume that this prim *pâtisserie* and tea salon is just one of the area's many mediocre eateries that cater to the hordes of undiscriminating tourists. The meticulously arranged windows displaying the house cakes, candies, and beautifully fashioned *pâtes d'amandes* (French marzipan), however, will reassure you that you can actually have a thoroughly enjoyable (and tranquil) meal at Maison Cador, which has been in business since shortly after Claude Monet stood on the facing museum balcony in 1867 to paint the church of Saint-Germain-l'Auxerrois that stands next door.

A dozen or so antique, marble-topped wooden tables with delicate caned chairs and benches fill two modest-sized gold-and-cream rooms made grand by elaborate gilded relief work and gleaming crystal chandeliers. Alongside a smattering of casually attired Louvre visitors are the tea salon's main customers—fashionable older, wool-suited ladies (and the occasional gentleman) who have been lunching here for decades. Some of them tuck into an artfully arranged *salade niçoise* or one of the restaurant's several quiches and omelets; some sip champagne while enjoying the rhubarb tart, an *éclair*, or one of the dozens of other sweets, including ice creams, that are made on the premises.

Pharamond

24, RUE DE LA GRANDE TRUANDERIE (1ST ARR.)
01.40.28.03.00
MÉTRO: HALLES
NOON-2:30PM & 7:30PM-10:00PM
CLOSED SUNDAY & MONDAY LUNCH

✦

THE SMALL PARIS NEIGHBORHOOD, BEAU-
BOURG, NOW THE HOME OF THE POMPIDOU
Center, originally took its name from a humorous
allusion to the enormous mound of refuse that was
dumped here by the adjoining food market of Les
Halles. Today, the so-called "beautiful borough"
bears little resemblance to its former self since the
removal of the wholesale vendors to the suburbs
several decades ago. On a street named for the
vagrants who once lived off the dump in this still
frankly seedy area is one of the few holdouts from
the early days. Pharamond, which specializes in the
cuisine of Normandy, has tenaciously held its
ground here since 1832.

Entering from these drab environs, the restau-
rant's lovely interior remains an unexpected pleasure.
Just twenty years after it relocated to this site,
Pharamond was redecorated in the latest Art

Nouveau style in preparation for the Universal Exposition of 1900. Above the upholstered banquettes and vintage bentwood chairs, mirrors are set in a kaleidoscope of turquoise, yellow, lavender, and pale-green *pâte-de-verre* panels that feature branches of apple trees, one of Normandy's principal crops. Just beneath the ceiling is a frieze of carrots, potatoes, and other vegetables that might appear in the brimming copper pots that are still brought to the tables holding some of the restaurant's signature dishes; the *tripes à la mode de Caen* (a stew of beef tripe and vegetables slowly cooked in cider and Calvados) once was sold from a horse-drawn cart on the streets of Paris by Pharamond's original owner.

The low-key friendly staff that work in his restaurant today also offer starters such as lobster ravioli, leeks *vinaigrette*, and the *Salade Folle*—greens topped with *haricots verts*, *foie gras*, and *magret de canard*—and main courses such as *coquilles St-Jacques au cidre* (sea scallops in cider), veal medallions, and grilled salmon. Among the desserts are *profiteroles*, *quatre quart* (pound cake), and *crêpes normandes*, with apples flambéed in Calvados.

La Potée des Halles

3, RUE ÉTIENNE-MARCEL (1ST ARR.)
01.40.41.98.15
MÉTRO: ÉTIENNE-MARCEL
NOON-2:30PM & 7PM-10:30PM
CLOSED SATURDAY LUNCH & SUNDAY

✦

LA POTÉE DES HALLES BEGAN ITS LIFE AT THE TURN OF THE LAST CENTURY AS ONE of the scores of modest cafés and *bistros* on the fringe of the central food market that served as canteens for the hard-working laborers who made their living provisioning the city. Although the fare these places served was decidedly simple by the standards of the grand palaces of gastronomy, they could boast that their proximity to the great iron-and-glass wholesale food pavilions assured their customers the freshest ingredients in all of Paris.

The focal point of La Potée des Halles are the faience-tile murals that depict two lovely maidens— one personifying beer, the other coffee—on the walls above the brown-leather banquettes and the old zinc-topped bar. Completing the decor are a stained-glass partition with lilies of the valley, large beveled mirrors, and vintage copper pots—a reference to the dish of the *bistro's* name, a robust stew from the Auvergne. The *potée* here is made from the restaurant's original 1903 recipe, with salt pork, smoked sausage, carrots, cabbage, and white beans.

Within this charming period interior, large parties of young, casually dressed diners crowd in for a menu that combines old-style favorites like the *potée* with more inventive, contemporary fare: a *gratin* of avocado and *roquefort*, a fish soup, herring fillets, braised salmon with sorrel sauce, *confit* of duck with sauteed potatoes, and for dessert, *île flottante*, chocolate mousse, and a red-berry *charlotte*.

À la Tour de Montlhéry

CHEZ DENISE

5, RUE DES PROUVAIRES (1ST ARR.)
01.42.36.21.82
MÉTRO: LOUVRE-RIVOLI
7AM MONDAY-7AM SATURDAY
CLOSED SATURDAY & SUNDAY

✦

THIS CASUAL AND LIVELY LES HALLES LAND-MARK HAS BEEN IN BUSINESS FOR MORE than 150 years, replacing a coach inn that had been housed in the half-timbered eighteenth-century building since the years following the French Revolution. In the early seventeenth century, the small street was the birthplace of Cyrano de Bergerac.

Just inside the restaurant, one encounters aged hams and sausages hanging from the wooden rafters and large stacked barrels that store the house Beaujolais. The stone walls are a nicotine-stained putty color; the old floor is a simple patterned tile with a trap door behind the zinc bar that leads to an ancient underground passage. A slate board chalked with the day's offerings is quickly brought to the long, communal tables covered with white paper over red-checked cloths. Despite the fact that this street was once part of the vegetable and fruit market (produce farmers from the village of Montlhéry south of Paris often ate here), the restaurant specializes in meat and *abats* (organs). Even fish may be prepared like a *boeuf bourguignon*, arriving in a thick, red wine-enhanced sauce studded with pearl onions and mushrooms. This is the hearty fare that once sustained the back-breaking labor of the farmers and the *forts des Halles*, the licensed market porters who pushed the enormous, food-laden carts throughout the stalls: rough country *pâté, steak frites, pot-au-feu*, lamb with white beans, veal kidneys, tripe, *lapin à la moutarde*. Desserts such as *oeufs à la neige, baba au rhum, mousse au chocolat*, and *crème caramel* round out the meal.

Maintaining tradition, La Tour de Montlhéry is closed on the weekends but otherwise stays open throughout the night, during what were once the market's and the restaurant's busiest hours.

L'Arbre à Cannelle

57, PASSAGE DES PANORAMAS (2ND ARR.)
01.45.08.55.87
MÉTRO: GRANDS BOULEVARDS
11:30AM–6PM; CLOSED SUNDAY

✦

IN 1817, THIS COVERED PEDESTRIAN ARCADE OFF THE GRANDS BOULEVARDS WAS THE first passage in the capital to be illuminated by gaslight. Parisians flocked here to see the spectacular panoramas, large-scale circular paintings that had been devised by the colorful American inventor Robert Fulton at the end of the eighteenth century to completely surround spectators and create the illusion of standing within dramatic scenes from history or amid the exotic landscapes of far-away lands.

Although the panoramas are long gone, the passage still boasts several nineteenth-century businesses—among them Stern, a stationer operating at no. 47 since 1840. A former *chocolatier*'s surviving façade still bears its old name, À la Caravanne, along with images of palm trees and camels, and a list of the exotic delicacies that it once carried. Picking up on that theme, L'Arbre à Cannelle (the cinnamon tree) is the name of the casual tea salon that now operates in these somewhat worn premises. Set out beside panels of carved wooden rosettes and Corinthian columns are a few marble-topped tables and wicker chairs in the passage itself. Inside, under an elaborate wooden ceiling, the mostly young customers from nearby offices lunch on a variety of *salades composées*, eggs, or savory tarts such as the *provençal* (tomatoes, eggplant, peppers, zucchini, and olives), *maraichère* (mushrooms, spinach, and leeks), and *fromagerie* (goat cheese and watercress). Sweets include ice creams, *sorbets*, and *tartes sucrées*, made with berries, apples, or pears. In addition to wines, coffee, hot chocolate, and teas, L'Arbre à Cannelle prepares a variety of fresh fruit cocktails.

Café le Croissant

146, RUE MONTMARTRE (2ND ARR.)
01.42.33.35.04
MÉTRO: SÉNTIER
6:30AM-9:00PM
MEALS SERVED 11:30AM-3:30PM
CLOSED SATURDAY & SUNDAY

✦

A SMALL PAINTING IN THE MUSÉE CARNAVALET, THE MUSEUM DEVOTED TO THE HISTORY of Paris, shows a boisterous group of old-time newsboys with the latest edition emerging from the rue du Croissant, a side street in the heart of the city's newspaper district in the second *arrondissement*. Visible at the side of the picture is the Café du Croissant, which has been in business at the corner of the rue Montmartre since 1850, and was itself the center of a news storm in 1914, when Jean Jaurès, a popular socialist politician opposed to the looming conflict with Germany, was assassinated while he was dining here.

Apart from a large marble plaque outside the café and, inside, a glass case that contains a bust of the slain leader and other items commemorating that historic event, the place is indistinguishable from the many other busy cafés and *bistros* in the area that still cater to lunching journalists along with financial types from the nearby Paris stock exchange. With slender interior columns that have been faced with small mirrored tiles and other questionable twentieth-century additions, little remains of Le Croissant's original decor. Nonetheless, the loyal regular patrons continue to come for straightforward hot and cold café fare that includes various composed salads, salmon (cooked, *tartare*, and *carpaccio*), tuna steak, *entrecôte bordelaise*, and steak *tartare*.

Café Runtz

16, RUE FAVART (2ND ARR.)
01.42.96.69.86
MÉTRO: RICHELIEU-DROUOT
9AM-11:30PM
CLOSED SATURDAY LUNCH & SUNDAY

✦

BY THE END OF THE NINETEENTH CENTURY, THERE WAS AN AVERAGE OF ONE CAFÉ occupying every other building in this busy central quarter off the *grands boulevards*. Runtz, an Alsatian café already in business for several decades by that time, is one of a handful from the period still operating. Not a café proper, and considerably less boisterous than the average Alsatian *brasserie*, Runtz offers the region's popular specialties to area business people at lunch and to theater-goers at night: duck *foie gras*, salad topped with *gruyère* and sausage, *quiche Lorraine*, warm potato salad with pork knuckles, onion tart, and five *choucroute* platters that are typically washed down with either an Alsatian beer or the house Riesling. The restaurant also offers a late-afternoon tea service with Alsatian pastries.

The welcoming decor is also more sedate than that of the average stained-glass-and-faience palaces that house most *brasseries*, essentially limited to a cheerful green-and-white checked fabric for the upholstery and curtains, little red-silk shades on the table lamps and chandeliers, and assorted decorative blue-and-white rustic crockery on display. The walls are covered with large mirrors and murals that depict scenes from various productions at the Salle Favart across the street, home in the nineteenth century to the Opéra Comique, whose Italian troupe of performers gave their name to the boulevard des Italiens at the corner.

Drouant

16, PLACE GAILLON (2ND ARR.)
01.42.65.15.16
MÉTRO: 4-SEPTEMBRE OR OPÉRA
NOON-2:30PM & 7PM-10:30PM DAILY

✦

ÉMILE ZOLA SET THE ACTION OF HIS 1882 NOVEL, "THE LADIES PARADISE," AN ACCOUNT of the rise of the new Parisian department stores, in the place Gaillon, a quiet backwater near the Opéra. Two years earlier, Charles Drouant, an Alsatian who had settled in the city after the Franco-Prussian war, opened a restaurant specializing in seafood on the same small *place*.

Zola knew the establishment well, and it quickly became popular with many of the artists in his circle, including Renoir, Rodin, and Monet, who for a time organized regular Friday night suppers at Drouant with friends such as Georges Clemenceau and Edmond de Goncourt; the prestigious French literary prize that is awarded in Goncort's honor has been decided at an annual dinner in the upstairs dining room here since 1914. When he wasn't slumming in the bawdy cafés and cabarets of Montmartre, Toulouse-Lautrec was also a frequent Drouant diner.

The elegant pale-grey lacquer façade, simply adorned with the restaurant's name in gold script, gives onto a grand Art Deco interior that the owner installed in the early 1920s. Here, or beneath canvas umbrellas on the private, shrubbery-enclosed sidewalk terrace, a combination of classic and contemporary preparations is served to a sophisticated Parisian business crowd. The menu features fish soup with saffron, *ratatouille* topped with a poached egg, *terrine* of *rouget* (red mullet) and crab, grilled shrimp with lemon and ginger, curried baby lamb, lobster with garlic and *cèpes*, *baba au rhum*, *île flottante*, and assorted *sorbets* prepared with seasonal fruits.

Gallopin

40, RUE NOTRE-DAME-DES-VICTOIRES
(2ND ARR.)
01.42.36.45.38
MÉTRO: BOURSE
NOON-3PM & 7PM-12:30AM
CLOSED SATURDAY LUNCH & SUNDAY

✦

THIS IS A BUSINESS-LIKE PLACE THAT HAS CATERED TO SUCCESSIVE GENERATIONS OF businesspeople who have lunched here since Gustave Gallopin opened his *brasserie* in 1876 in the heart of the financial and newspaper district. Not surprisingly, the restaurant is best visited at midday, when it hums with deal-making and animated chatter. But unlike many of the older Parisian establishments that look as if they have not been painted or polished in decades, this place is sparkling—gleaming frosted glass panels, beveled mirrors, brass railings, and copper beer pumps.

Gallopin's front room is dominated by a burnished Cuban mahogany *bar Americaine* and is consciously English Victorian in feel; the back room, with its delicately colored stained-glass panels and faience tiles, feels more French Art Nouveau. The

[41]

proper black-vested, white-aproned waiters bustle around delivering starters of haddock *carpaccio*, *haricots verts*, prosciutto and melon, the house duck *pâté*, and main-course *plats* of sauteed sole, grilled bass with fennel, roast cod, braised veal, and a vegetarian plate. The *aperitif belle époque* is made with Lillet. In fair weather, several tables placed outside face the back of Napoleon's neoclassical temple to commerce, the 1826 Paris Stock Exchange building.

Le Grand Colbert

2, RUE VIVIENNE (2ND ARR.)
01.42.86.87.88
MÉTRO: BOURSE
NOON-1AM DAILY

✦

IN THE DAYS WHEN PARIS WAS STILL LARGELY AN UNPAVED CITY, REFINED VISITORS TO THE galerie Vivienne could have the mud removed from their boots and the dust from their clothes at the enterprising *salon de décrottage*. Newly freshened, they would proceed to the prestigious shops and restaurants located within the vaulted, Pompeian-style arcade that had been erected in 1823, just north of the Palais-Royal gardens. Along with the oldest bookstore in Paris, Le Grand Colbert is among the few of those early-nineteenth-century businesses to have survived within the galleries. Named for the finance minister of Louis XIV who had lived in the same building, the restaurant has entrances on both the rue Vivienne and within the galerie Colbert, a smaller passage that sits nestled within the L-shaped galerie Vivienne.

Modern visitors to the landmarked restaurant will find a heavily restored period decor with large globe lights surrounding the columns that divide the high-ceilinged dining room, an intricately tiled mosaic floor, and a frieze of painted neoclassical panels. In addition to oysters and other chilled shellfish from an extensive raw bar, Le Grand Colbert offers lentil salad, *haricot verts* with *foie gras*, *escargots*, steak *tartare*, roast lamb with *gratin dauphinois*, salmon with sorrel, *lotte* (monkfish) in a saffron sauce, lamb curry, and a large selection of traditional desserts. Afternoon tea, featuring a hot chocolate *de la maison*, is also available.

Legrand Filles et Fils

1, RUE DE LA BANQUE (2ND ARR.)
01.42.60.07.12
MÉTRO: BOURSE OR PALAIS-ROYAL
9AM-7:30PM
8:30AM-1PM & 3PM-7PM SATURDAY
CLOSED SUNDAY & MONDAY

✦

AMONG THE SOBER, NEARLY IDENTICAL LIME-STONE BUILDINGS THAT DOMINATE THIS commercial section of central Paris near the Palais-Royal and the old Bibliothèque Nationale, the cheerful Bordeaux-red storefront of this picturesque, top-quality *épicerie* has stood out for the three generations that the Legrand family has owned it. Inside, the original wooden display shelves continue to offer jars of *confiture*, tins of old-fashioned French candies, boxes of cookies, crackers, coffees, and teas, as they have since 1890. Almost all of the merchandise here would make appealing gifts and souvenirs that are both relatively inexpensive and easy to transport.

The shop floor is the usual attractive patterned tile of the period; the ceiling, a most unusual mosaic made up of hundreds of wine corks. The back room opens onto the neoclassical galerie Vivienne, one of only twenty of the elegant early-nineteenth-century covered shopping arcades known as *passages* to have survived. Here, wines—particularly from some of the smaller, less well-known French vineyards—*aperitifs*, Cognacs, Armagnacs, and various *eaux-de-vie*—are featured along with wine glasses, corkscrews, decanters, carafes, and other useful articles for the serious oenophile.

Legend has it that the extensive *caves* beneath Legrand were once the catacombs of the nearby Notre-Dame-des-Victoires.

Aux Lyonnais

32, RUE SAINT-MARC (2ND ARR.)
01.42.96.65.04
MÉTRO: BOURSE, RICHELIEU-DROUOT,
OR 4-SEPTEMBRE
NOON-2:30PM & 7PM-11:30PM
CLOSED SATURDAY LUNCH, SUNDAY & AUGUST

✦

AUX LYONNAIS, WITH ITS GLOSSY DEEP-RED FAÇADE, HAS OPERATED FOR MORE THAN a century as a homey, unpretentious haven in the center of the hectic commercial heart of the city. Inside, the creamy white walls are embellished with large beveled mirrors, garlands sculpted in high-relief stucco, and a frieze of roses painted on enameled tiles. The restaurant's windows are covered with traditional white-lace café curtains, and old-style globe lights hang from the ceiling.

In this classic *bistro* interior, diners feast on classic *bistro* fare, much of it specialties from the city of Lyon. All are served in copious, larger-than-usual portions, with main courses that come to the table with a side dish of cooked vegetables and three different preparations of potato. Sausage with warm potatoes dressed in olive oil, tossed green salad topped with chicken livers, and a fish *terrine* are typical of the hearty starters. These may be followed by *plats du jour* such as *canard au poivre* (duck fillet with a green-peppercorn sauce), rabbit with shallots, *boeuf gros sel* (boiled beef served with vegetables and coarse salt), *poule au pot* (chicken in cream with mushrooms and tarragon), or *coquilles Saint-Jacques* (sea scallops) in either a *rémoulade* or *provençal* sauce. For dessert, offerings include *poire Belle Héléne*, *poire cardinal*, coffee or *chocolat liegeois*.

Au Panetier

10, PLACE DES PETITS-PÈRES (2ND ARR.)
01.42.60.90.23
MÉTRO: BOURSE
8AM-7:15PM; CLOSED SATURDAY & SUNDAY

✦

IN DIRECT CONTRAST TO THE AUSTERE FAÇADE OF THE EIGHTEENTH-CENTURY church of Notre-Dame-des-Victoires that it faces, the delightful Belle Epoque *boulangerie* Au Panetier is a riot of Art Nouveau decorative elements. The bake shop's own façade, adorned with sinuous dark-green letters and *nouille* (noodle-style) woodwork gives onto a multicolored L-shaped interior embellished with globe lights, etched-glass panels, a painted ceiling set in a sculpted stucco border, and large tile murals of exotic birds and branches of flowering plum and cherry trees.

First thing in the morning, at lunchtime, and again as people head home from work, lines form outside the shop as Panetier's regular customers stop by for their *pain quotidien* (daily bread). The loaves are baked every day at dawn in century-old, wood-fired ovens in the building's cellar, using eight different types of dough. Many varieties of cookies, cakes, and tarts, pre-made sandwiches on several types of bread, single-serving *quiches*, and chocolates can also be purchased along with canned and bottled drinks; these can make a lovely picnic that can be consumed in the splendid gardens of the Palais-Royal, a two-minute walk from here.

Specialty loaves of bread in a variety of unusual shapes and sizes may be ordered in advance.

Stohrer

51, RUE MONTORGUEIL (2ND ARR.)
01.42.33.38.20
MÉTRO: HALLES
7:30AM-8:30PM; CLOSED MONDAY

✦

STOHRER BEARS THE DISTINCT HONOR OF
BEING THE OLDEST PÂTISSERIE IN PARIS
as well as a national historic monument. The
eponymous founder was a French baker in the service of the Polish king who returned to his native
country with Princess Marie when she arrived to
marry Louis XV. Monsieur Stohrer remained at
Versailles with the royals for just five years before
setting up shop in 1730 on the rue Montorgueil,
now as then, one of the most animated market
streets leading to Les Halles.

Beneath a delicately painted ceiling that evokes
fine French porcelain, murals of two ethereal
maidens—one holding a sheaf of wheat, the other
several small cakes—face one another across the
narrow shop. Set out on glass display shelves, the
baked goods include the *baba au rhum*, which
Stohrer is credited with inventing, *charlottes*, *petits-
fours*, and the colorful *tarte aux sept fruits*, with its

strawberries, raspberries, peaches, tangerines, pears, kiwi, and fig.

When Stohrer first opened, few ordinary Parisians had ovens in their homes, so birds and other meats would be brought to *boulangeries* and *pâtisseries*, where, for a small fee, they were roasted. This service finds an echo in today's shop, which also operates as a *traiteur* (caterer), with various composed salads and sandwiches of curried chicken, *roquefort* and nuts, crab, *foie gras*, and smoked salmon, among others, available to take out. These can be taken down the street to the gardens beside the underground shopping complex that now occupies Les Halles.

FOURTH

ARRONDISSEMENT

✦

Bofinger

5-7, RUE DE LA BASTILLE (4TH ARR.)
01.42.72.87.82
MÉTRO: BASTILLE
NOON-3PM & 6:30PM-1AM MONDAY-FRIDAY
NOON-1AM SATURDAY & SUNDAY

✦

PARISIANS DID NOT BEGIN TO DRINK BEER IN SIGNIFICANT QUANTITIES UNTIL THE middle of the nineteenth century, when the beverage's association with peasants made it popular following the revolution of 1848. Originally, *brasseurs* (brewers), gave their name to only those establishments that served beer. More recently, *brasseries* have tended to distinguish themselves as ornate larger restaurants that provide meal service all day long, rather than closing the kitchen between the lunch and dinner hours. For this reason, they tend to specialize in simple foods that can be made rapidly or prepared ahead of time without the careful attention of a classically trained chef.

Whether or not Bofinger's claim is strictly true that it was the first place in the city to serve draft beer *à la pompe* (on tap), starting in 1864, the restaurant is considered by many to be the quintessential

[55]

Parisian *brasserie*. In these large, festive, two-story premises between the place de la Bastille and the place des Vosges, all the classic *brasserie* elements are in place: a beautifully maintained Belle Epoque decor with mirrored walls, tufted banquette seating, palms potted in colorful majolica urns, and stained glass in the form of an enormous cupola above the ground-floor dining room. The various ranks of waiters are traditionally attired; the specialties are onion soup, traditional *choucroutes*, grilled fish and meats, and elaborately tiered presentations of briny, fresh shellfish.

Brasserie de l'Ile St-Louis

55, QUAI DE BOURBON (4TH ARR.)
01.43.54.02.59
MÉTRO: PONT-MARIE
NOON-1AM; CLOSED WEDNESDAY & AUGUST

✦

MANY OF THE MOST VENERATED FRENCH ARTISTS AND WRITERS—ZOLA, SAND, Voltaire, Balzac, Daumier, Courbet, Baudelaire, Delacroix, and Cézanne—at one time chose to live on the village-like Ile-Saint-Louis, the smaller of the two Seine islands that has always been a tranquil oasis in the center of the busy city. Although the island is much changed, some of its oldest businesses are still operating today; the restaurant on the western tip, like so many *brasseries* in Paris, dates from around 1870.

The loss to Germany of Alsace-Lorraine that year following the Franco-Prussian war sent many of the province's citizens to the capital in search of a new life that often included opening restaurants featuring their hearty regional cuisine. In contrast to the city's glittering larger *brasseries*, the mounted animal heads here, along with the rustic lighting fixtures fashioned from wooden barrels and folk-art

[57]

scenes painted on the windows are typical of more modest establishments where the decorations are simply disparate objects acquired over many decades. The large copper espresso maker behind the bar is reputed to be the oldest one still working in Paris.

The specialty is still that Alsatian staple, *choucroute garnie*, both the standard version of sauerkraut garnished with ham, bacon, and pork loin, and a less traditional fish *choucroute* prepared with smoked haddock. These are served with either a regional beer in heavy clay mugs or chilled Alsatian Riesling in the traditional green-stemmed wine glasses; little pots of caraway seeds sit beside the salt, pepper, and mustard on the communal tables that fill the small dining hall. This is a great place to come with a crowd for leeks *vinaigrette*, herring with potatoes, Welsh rarebit, steak (grilled or *tartare*) *coq-au-Riesling*, *poule faisanne* (pheasant hen), omelets (with Alsatian muenster cheese), onion tart, and salads.

Tables on the outside terrace overlook the Seine and the apse of Notre-Dame cathedral on the Ile de la Cité.

Chez Julien

1, RUE DU PONT LOUIS-PHILIPPE (4TH ARR.)
01.42.78.31.64
MÉTRO: PONT-MARIE
NOON–2PM & 7:30PM–11PM
CLOSED SUNDAY & MONDAY LUNCH

✦

FOR THE PAST FEW DECADES, HISTORIC PREMISES, PROTECTED IN FRANCE AS national monuments, have been increasingly rescued, recycled, and refitted for entirely new lives in modern Paris. Belle Epoque *épiceries* have become fine restaurants, Art Nouveau *pâtisseries* are refashioned into exclusive boutiques, and, in the case of Chez Julien, two nineteenth-century shops, a bar and a *boulangerie,* were joined to become home to a charming corner *bistro.*

On one side of the landmarked façade remains the circa-1820 grillwork of the former bar; on the other side, the bakery's pastoral landscapes painted under glass have been preserved. A sepia-toned photograph that hangs in the intimate, dimly lit dining room shows turn-of-the-century shoppers crossing in front of the two tiny stores. A hundred years later, their combined intact interiors still feature a front room with the elaborate old oak bar and a second room adorned with fanciful floating cherubs, peasant maidens, harvest scenes, and sheaves of wheat. In good weather, tables are also available on the picturesque terraced cobblestone street alongside the restaurant that face a stunning view of the Seine, the Ile de la Cité, and the Ile Saint-Louis. Diners can choose starters from a menu that features *profiteroles* of snails with a tarragon sauce, *fricassée* of mushrooms, and duck *foie gras* with champagne. Main courses include medallions of veal with mushrooms, duck *à l'orange*, and sea scallops with white wine, basil, and garlic. Among other sweets, the house dessert is *fraises à la Romanoff* (strawberries in Cointreau and Grand Marnier).

Mariage Frères

30-32, RUE DU BOURG-TIBOURG (4TH ARR.)
01.42.72.28.11
MÉTRO: ST-PAUL OR HÔTEL-DE-VILLE
LUNCH: NOON-4PM MONDAY-FRIDAY
TEA: 3PM-7PM MONDAY-FRIDAY
BRUNCH: NOON-6PM SATURDAY & SUNDAY
SHOP: 10:30AM-7:30PM DAILY

✦

IN 1854, ROUGHLY TWO CENTURIES AFTER THE INTRODUCTION OF TEA TO FRANCE during the reign of Louis XIV, the Mariage brothers— Henri and Edouard—founded this enduring tea importing business, now the oldest *maison de thé* in the country. Although there are several outposts elsewhere in the city, this original location on the Right Bank in the Marais has grown to include a combination retail shop, tea room, as well as an eccentric little tea museum.

On the perpetually crowded ground floor, customers and staff treat the selection of 450 brews from some three dozen countries with the seriousness of choosing a fine wine. In the rear colonial-style dining-room, tea (always prepared at Mariage Frères with filtered water) may accompany fresh fruit juice and muffins with tea jelly at brunch; at lunch, it joins salads or savory hot plates; and at afternoon tea time, it's served with one of the delicate house desserts, including a tea-flavored *crème brûlée*. Above the fray, in the charming upstairs *musée du thé*, are lovely antique tea services, caddies, tea balls, and other tea-related accoutrements. A wicker hamper holds a portable tea-for-two picnic, with a sterno-warmed pot, cups, saucers, and linen napkins.

In addition to the loose tea leaves and teas bagged in little muslin sachets, the boutique, one of the most elegant shops of its kind in Paris, also sells a large selection of finely crafted *théières* (tea pots) specifically designed for various blends, beautifully colored canisters, tea-scented cookies, and sugars that make excellent gifts to bring home.

À l'Olivier

23, RUE DE RIVOLI (4TH ARR.)
01.48.04.86.59
MÉTRO: ST-PAUL OR HÔTEL-DE-VILLE
9:30AM-1PM & 2PM-7PM
CLOSED SUNDAY & MONDAY

✦

THIS VENERABLE PURVEYOR OF FINE OILS NEAR THE PLACE DES VOSGES IN THE Marais was already forty-five years old when it was awarded, at the 1867 Universal Exposition, the medals of excellence that are still proudly displayed in the front windows. Of course there are quantities of extra virgin olive oil from five different countries, as well as the usual safflower, sunflower, and corn oil, but there are also cooking and salad oils that have been pressed from grape, pumpkin, and sesame seeds, wheat germ, walnuts, hazelnuts, and almonds as well as many specially flavored varieties. Where there is oil, there must be vinegar—red, white, balsamic, cider, sherry, champagne, raspberry, garlic, and pepper, among others.

Also available at l'Olivier are more than a dozen selections of glistening black and green *provençal* olives, as well as *tapenades*, mustards, *cornichons*, capers, fragrant dried herbs, and *fleur de sel*, the premium French sea salt that is harvested on the Atlantic coast; open burlap bags display great quantities of black, white, green, and red peppercorns. Among the inedible wares: olivewood salad bowls and bread boards, cruets, *torchons* (dish towels) that are decorated with olive branches, oil-based soaps, scented shampoos, and body lotions.

Framed sepia-toned photographs of the shop at the turn of the last century and during the Great Depression reveal how little the *huilerie* has changed throughout the many decades.

Au Petit Fer à Cheval

30, RUE VIEILLE-DU-TEMPLE (4TH ARR.)
01.42.72.47.47
MÉTRO: HÔTEL-DE-VILLE
7AM–2AM DAILY

✦

A LTHOUGH IT HAD ONCE BEEN THE HEIGHT
OF FASHION, THE MARAIS EVENTUALLY
was abandoned by aristocratic eighteenth-century
Parisians for newly stylish districts on the other side
of the city. The eastern Right Bank quarter fell into a
long period of decline from which it did not recover
for nearly two hundred years. Honoré de Balzac,
who attended school in what is now the Picasso
museum, described the area in his day as a veritable
wilderness; Victor Hugo, who lived nearby at 6,
place des Vosges (now the Hugo museum), placed a
nest of dangerous outlaws in the passage des Signes
off the once-grand rue Vieille-du-Temple. Today, just
down the street from that notorious alley is a modest
turn-of-the-century café that has held its ground as
the pendulum's backswing has forced most of the
small factories, auto-repair shops, and working-class
eateries from the noble *hôtels particuliers* into which
they had settled.

Au Petit Fer à Cheval, named for the beautiful horseshoe-shaped bar that dominates the deep, narrow front room, is one of the most popular spots in the very hip twenty-first-century Marais. Outside, beneath the old lettering that has survived for decades on the original façade, a few marble-topped café tables and chairs claim several square feet of the ever-crowded pavement. In the little back room, hot meals such as duck *confit* or filet mignon of veal are listed on a chalkboard and available all day at the dozen small wooden booths, along with steak *tartare*, assortments of *charcuterie* or cheese, sandwiches and salads, such as the *fer à cheval*, mixed greens topped with *haricots verts*, sliced raw mushrooms, and warmed goat cheese.

.)

O "OLD
GEWAY
d to the
. directly
about the
ble decor
s for more

than a hun—

When the *bistro* ope— rs following
Napoleon III and Baron Haussmann's massive recon-
figuration of Paris, only a few hundred people were
left inhabiting the newly cleaned-up Ile de la Cité,
which long had been one of the city's most crowded
and miserable slums. To this day, the area has
remained largely an administrative center and tends
to be rather deserted at night. At lunchtime, however,
you leave a very busy street of souvenir shops and
tour buses for the calm of the *bistro's* small, dark
front room, where regulars are seated opposite the

old wooden bar; a larger, brighter room in the back serves most newcomers, many of them foreign tourists. Both groups come to this unlikely location for the house *andouillette* (chitterlings sausage), the *boudins*, and *terrines*, and for the *boeuf bourguignon*, deemed one of the best in the city. For fish lovers, there are mussels that arrive sizzling in little pools of melted butter, Baltic herring, and *coquilles Saint-Jacques* (sea scallops) in a whiskey-and-cream sauce. The *tarte tatin*, one of many traditional desserts, is served flambéed with Calvados.

FIFTH

ARRONDISSEMENT

✦

Brasserie Balzar

49, RUE DES ÉCOLES (5TH ARR.)
01.43.54.13.67
MÉTRO: CLUNY-SORBONNE
NOON-MIDNIGHT DAILY

✦

AS FAR BACK AS THE MIDDLE AGES, THE LATIN QUARTER ON THE LEFT BANK HAS BEEN home to countless taverns and inns that catered exclusively to the students and scholars of the Sorbonne and other nearby colleges. Among the current sea of indifferent student cafés and inexpensive eateries in what is still the university neighborhood of modern Paris, only a very few establishments have endured longer than a generation or two.

One important exception, however, is Brasserie Balzar, whose classic Art Deco interior of red-leather banquette seating, mirrored walls, and simple tile flooring, conceals the true age of this small but always bustling landmark restaurant. The *brasserie* first opened on the broad rue des Ecoles near the Musée Cluny, the museum of medieval art, in the late 1890s, making it a rarity—a Latin Quarter centenarian. To dine here today is to participate in a real Paris institution. In fact, the establishment is so beloved by its habitués that a committee was formed to protect the place against any unwelcome "improvements" dreamed up by its new management, a restaurant group with large holdings in the city. Few changes have made their way onto Balzar's classic menu, which is available throughout the day and features onion soup *gratinée*, celery root *rémoulade*, herring with warm potatoes, *mâche* salad with beets, steak *tartare*, roast chicken, sautéed calf's liver, *tarte tatin*, *profiteroles*, and *crème caramel*.

Café service is available in the shallow glass-enclosed terrace that overlooks the busy street.

La Tour d'Argent

17, QUAI DE LA TOURNELLE (5TH ARR.)
01.43.54.23.31
MÉTRO: MAUBERT-MUTUALITÉ
OR CARDINAL LEMOINE
NOON-2:30PM & 7:30PM-10:30PM
CLOSED MONDAY

✦

LEGEND MAINTAINS THAT AS LONG AGO AS THE SIXTEENTH CENTURY, AN INN WHERE the fork is said to have been introduced to Paris operated on this site of the Left Bank riverfront. In 1780, a restaurant, then a novelty in the city, opened here, only to be ransacked just nine years later by the revolutionary mob returning from storming the Bastille. Once re-established, it went on to serve such nineteenth-century luminaries as George Sand, Alexandre Dumas, Honoré de Balzac, and Emperor Napoleon III.

Today, La Tour d'Argent, renowned for its stunning penthouse view of Notre-Dame cathedral, may be the very model of the legendary historic restaurant that continues to draw crowds (predominantly foreign tourists, however) despite the near universal disregard among critics and natives for the quality of both its cuisine and service—especially considering the heft of its prices. The signature dish remains the famed *canard au sang*, the duck that has been tortuously extracted from a specially designed press. Each bird still arrives at the table bearing a numbered card, an ingenious marketing ploy instituted roughly 900,000 ducks ago in 1890 when the recipe was devised. Other specialties at this most traditional of classic French restaurants include pheasant *consommé*, filet of *sole Cardinal* (with crayfish), *quenelles de brochet* (pike dumplings), a *millefeuille* with red berries, flambéed peaches, and *crèpes belle époque*.

Recalling the days when nineteenth-century merchants from the nearby wine market would gather here, La Tour d'Argent's half-million-bottle wine cellar, an ancient *cave* beneath the street, is considered among the city's finest.

SIXTH

ARRONDISSEMENT

✦

Le Bistro de la Gare

59, BOULEVARD MONTPARNASSE (6TH ARR.)
01.45.48.38.01
MÉTRO: MONTPARNASSE-BIENVENUE
DAILY UNTIL 1AM

✦

IN THE DECADES BEFORE IT ACHIEVED INTERNATIONAL RENOWN IN THE EARLY twentieth century as the center of the avant-garde art world, the Left Bank district of Montparnasse was a sleepy backwater. The district was centered on its rail depot, the Gare Montparnasse, then as now serving trains to and from Brittany, whose natives brought their regional cuisine to the neighborhood, which is still a center of Breton fish restaurants and *crèperies*. At the turn of the last century, the enterprising Chartier brothers, Camille and Edouard, purchased one such café near the railway station for their growing chain of inexpensive yet grandly designed eateries known as *bouillons*.

They new owners refitted the large premises with an exuberant Art Nouveau interior of undulating, pale-green woodwork, etched-globe lights, colored-glass-and-tile murals. What was then proudly declared the "modern style," is today registered among the national historic monuments.

The Bistro de la Gare is once again part of a chain of restaurants, its uninspired cuisine, unfortunately, as ordinary as its decor is extraordinary. For the most part, its patrons seem to be grabbing a quick meal—roast chicken with *pommes frites*, grilled meats and fish, and other standard fare— before catching a train or a film at one of the many boulevard Montparnasse multiplexes.

Bouillon Racine

3, RUE RACINE (6TH ARR.)
01.44.32.15.60
MÉTRO: CLUNY-SORBONNE OR ODÉON
11AM-12:30AM; 11AM-11PM SUNDAY

✦

IN 1996, WORK BEGAN ON THE PAINSTAKING TASK OF REVERSING NEARLY A CENTURY OF wear and tear to the Art Nouveau decor of this large restaurant housed in a building where George Sand had once lived. Each piece of *petit-crystal* was removed from the façade—one of the best preserved from the period—then numbered, restored, and eventually refitted. Inside the two-story restaurant, scores of beveled mirrors were reset into the sinuous frames of woodwork that had been returned to the original sprightly pale green. The one surviving patch of intricate mosaic floor tile was replicated throughout the premises. A repaired glass ceiling panel painted with flowers once again illuminates the framed *pâte-de-verre* panels that depict sunflowers, hydrangeas, lilies, hollyhocks, and flowering cherry branches.

Originally, the eatery was the Latin Quarter outpost of the Chartier chain of *bouillons* that catered to the Parisian middle class throughout the city. Now, Bouillon Racine's proximity to the boulevard Saint-Michel and the Sorbonne ensures a young crowd that comes to these pretty yet casual surroundings for the all-day service, the large selection of newspapers attached to wooden rods, and the live jazz in the evenings.

Despite the fact that the restaurant is listed as a French historic monument, the cuisine is now Belgian, a reflection of the current owner's pride in the food of his native land. Specialties include *waterzooi* (chicken and vegetables in cream), shrimp croquettes, *anguille au vert* (eels in a green sauce), Flemish preparations of lamb, Belgian waffles, and Belgian cheeses. Several dishes feature the unlikely pairing of Belgian gingerbread with, say, *tournedos* of salmon or eggplant caviar. The *carbonnade à la flamande* is a beef stew prepared with beer instead of red wine. Naturally, Belgian beer is the beverage of choice as well as the base of the unusual house *apéritifs du jour*. At tea time, a *pression* (draft beer), accompanies the daily specials on the *prix-fixe* menu. Even the mineral water served here is imported from Belgium.

Brasserie Lipp

151, BOULEVARD SAINT-GERMAIN (6TH ARR.)
01.45.48.53.91
MÉTRO: ST-GERMAIN
8AM-2AM DAILY

✦

WHEN ERNEST HEMINGWAY LOVINGLY DESCRIBED IN "A MOVEABLE FEAST" A meal that he had enjoyed at Brasserie Lipp during the 1920s, the Left Bank institution on the boulevard Saint-Germain had already been in business for more than forty years. Then, the restaurant's decor, with its painted ceilings, brass chandeliers, and faience tiles that depict exotic birds and plants, was only a few years old; today, it is a designated historic national monument.

Léonard Lipp and his wife were among the many Alsatian refugees who arrived in the capital to open small restaurants after their province was annexed to Germany following the Franco-Prussian war of 1870. Even though they named their new establishment after a renowned eatery in Strasbourg, the Brasserie des Bords du Rhin (On the Banks of the Rhine), Parisians insisted on calling it after the owners. Although the terrace has remained small by the standard of Café de Flore (page 83) and Aux Deux Magots (page 89), the two famous Saint-Germain cafés directly across the boulevard, Lipp eventually expanded into the building's courtyard and to a second-floor dining room that became the famous "Siberia" to which most foreigners and unknowns have typically been exiled.

Hemingway escaped that particular fate and was seated in the main room at one of the comfortable banquettes against the wall. His memorable feast consisted of *cervelas* (a garlicky pork sausage), potatoes marinated in olive oil, and a *sérieux* (a large stein of draft beer). These are all still available on the slender cardboard menu that admonishes in English: "No salad as a meal"—a reminder to modern-day Americans in Paris that this is a proper restaurant where one must order several courses. For starters, one might consider *foie gras*, smoked salmon, herring, or sardines, followed by one of the several varieties of *choucroute*, *cassoulet*, roast chicken, or steak *tartare*. The desserts include an Alsatian apple strudel, *profiteroles*, and a *millefeuille* that must be ordered at the beginning of the meal.

Café de Flore

172, BOULEVARD SAINT-GERMAIN (6TH ARR.)
01.45.48.55.26
MÉTRO: ST-GERMAIN
7:45AM-1:45AM DAILY

✦

LIKE AUX DEUX MAGOTS, ITS GREAT RIVAL A BLOCK AWAY, CAFÉ DE FLORE HAS BEEN a gathering place for writers since it opened in 1865 in this most literary Parisian neighborhood. As today, Saint-Germain in the nineteenth century was home to booksellers, bookbinders, publishers, and a veritable pantheon of acclaimed French writers. The young Victor Hugo lived in a garret at 30, rue du Dragon, the short street that begins across the boulevard Saint-Germain from the café; Honoré de Balzac worked as a book printer at 17, rue Visconti, a few blocks north of here in the house where Racine had died. George Sand moved to the nearby 31, rue de Seine after leaving her husband, and Gustave Flaubert resided at 20, rue de l'Odéon, a few blocks east of here. At the turn of the last century, Guillaume Apollinaire lived just down the boulevard at the corner of the rue du Pré-aux-Clercs.

Flore, which was named for a statue of the goddess of spring that then stood outside the building, sports the classic Art Deco redecoration it received between the two world wars, when it was the regular café of Left Bank intellectuals such as Pablo Picasso, Jean-Paul Sartre, and Simone de Beauvoir. Even today, when it attracts scores of guidebook-toting foreign tourists, hip locals (contemporary writers among them) continue to *rendezvous* here sipping espressos and *aperitifs*, enjoying eggs—scrambled, plain, or with ham and cheese, omelets, or *sur le plat* (fried)—Welsh rarebit, and salads, among them the *parisienne*, composed of *haricots verts*, shallots, and a choice of either *foie gras* or *magret de canard*.

Aux Charpentiers

10, RUE MABILLON (6TH ARR.)
01.43.26.30.05
MÉTRO: MABILLON
NOON-3PM & 7PM-11:30PM DAILY

✦

A RESTAURANT HAS EXISTED ON THIS SITE NEAR THE CHURCH OF SAINT-SULPICE since the middle of the nineteenth century and from 1874 under its present name. Then, this was the canteen of the neighboring carpenters' guild, whose members' virtuosic wooden scale models are still on proud display here, making the decor at Aux Charpentiers unique among the remaining Parisian *bistros* of the period.

Wood continues to dominate in the well-lit, informal dining room in the numerous framed prints and wainscotting, the unadorned plank floor, the vintage bentwood chairs and coatracks. At the turn of the last century, the woodworkers installed the long, carved oak bar by the restaurant's entrance; its zinc top is a modern copy of the original, which met the fate of so many in the city when it was confiscated during the Nazi Occupation of the Second World War, melted down, and turned into German arms.

Unfortunately, the traditional *bistro* fare at Charpentiers is sometimes prepared with a somewhat heavy hand: marinated herrings, poached sausage, warm potatoes in oil, stuffed cabbage, roast rabbit, braised beef, duck with olives and port wine, chocolate mousse, *tarte au citron*.

La Closerie des Lilas

171, BOULEVARD DU MONTPARNASSE (6TH ARR.)
01.43.26.70.50
MÉTRO: VAVIN OR PORT-ROYAL
BRASSERIE: 11:30AM-1AM DAILY
CAFÉ: 9AM-2AM DAILY
RESTAURANT: NOON-3PM & 7:30PM-11PM DAILY

✦

LOCATED ON THE LEFT BANK WHERE THE LATIN QUARTER MEETS MONTPARNASSE, is La Closerie des Lilas, a nineteenth-century establishment that found its real fame in the twentieth. In the 1920s, this was famously the "home café" of Ernest Hemingway, who put the finishing touches on "The Sun Also Rises" here while he was living around the corner at 113, rue Notre-Dame-des-Champs; the writer's memory is now enshrined on the printed menu, in several small brass plaques that mark his favorite seats, even on the small porcelain ashtrays.

The Closerie's long, circuitous history, however, dates back as far as the French Revolution, when it was an inn for stagecoach travelers. The scores of fragrant white and purple lilac bushes planted by one of its enterprising owners in the 1840s, when the site had become an open-air dance hall, eventually gave their name to the establishment's next incarnation, a café that came to include a *brasserie* and a more formal restaurant.

The heavy traffic that now passes on the boulevard Montparnasse vividly illustrates how much the area has changed since the Closerie opened. Remarkably, there were still vineyards, dairies, and fruit orchards surrounding the place when it counted among its regular customers notable painters (such as Ingres and Whistler) and writers (such as Chateaubriand and Balzac, who had a home on the rue Cassini near the Observatoire).

Oysters, *foie gras de canard*, grilled turbot, and steak *tartare* with *pommes frites* are among the classics served in the Art Deco dining rooms, though most people prefer the Closerie des Lilas for a *café-au-lait* on the shrubbery-enclosed terrace or for a drink at the bar.

Aux Deux Magots

170, BOULEVARD SAINT-GERMAIN (6TH ARR.)
01.45.48.55.25
MÉTRO: ST-GERMAIN
8AM-2AM DAILY

✦

IN 1813, THE OWNER OF A LEFT BANK LUXURY EMPORIUM—ONE OF THE FIRST OF ITS KIND in the city—took the name Les Deux Magots from the title of a popular theatrical piece of the day. The shop relocated to the place Saint-Germain in 1873, only to be replaced nine years later by a *café-liquoriste* whose proprietors decided to keep the familiar name as well as the distinctive wooden statues of the two Confucian wise men (*les deux magots*) that remain the focal point of the large main room.

That third incarnation has lasted the longest, Aux Deux Magots becoming one of the most celebrated cafés in Paris, if not the world. Although its real glory years, like that of Café Flore (page 83) down the street, date from its association with mid-twentieth-century writers, artists, and philosophers, the place has always attracted literary figures, with Verlaine, Rimbaud, and Mallarmé among the early habitués; the exiled Oscar Wilde, who spent the last year of his short life residing in a hotel on the nearby rue des Beaux-Arts, arrived here every morning for breakfast and returned again each evening for a glass of potent absinthe.

Nowadays, some guests sit in the staid, Art Deco interior, though most prefer the closely set marble-topped café tables and woven chairs on the famed terrace, part of which faces the frenetic activity of the boulevard, part of which looks out on the more serene cobblestone square in front of the lovely Saint-Germain-des-Prés, the oldest church in the city.

Mornings, *croissants*, *brioches*, and hard-cooked brown eggs are set out to tempt early visitors. Later in the day, light meals, including omelets, sandwiches, and salads (the *Deux Magots* is sliced ham, chicken breast, and tomatoes on a bed of lettuce) are brought to the table by the fleet of waiters traditionally attired in black jackets and floor-length white aprons. Whether the customers (generally deemed to include more foreign tourists than at Flore) are eating or simply lingering over a *café-au-lait*, a *citron pressé* (freshly squeezed lemonade), a *ballon* of Beaujolais, or a *kir*, the main activity of everyone at Deux Magots is people-watching.

Lapérouse

51, QUAI DES GRANDS-AUGUSTINS (6TH ARR.)
01.43.26.68.04
MÉTRO: PONT NEUF OR ST-MICHEL
12:15PM–2:30PM & 7PM–11PM
CLOSED MONDAY

✦

THE BUILDINGS THAT STAND ALONG THE LEFT BANK OF THE SEINE FACING THE Ile de la Cité are now among the oldest in Paris, having escaped the clean sweep of Napoleon III's epic urban renewal in the nineteenth century. Structures dating from the seventeenth and eighteenth centuries are not unusual on the narrow, winding streets of Saint-Germain-des-Prés, among them the house at 7, rue des Grands-Augustins, where Honoré de Balzac set the action of his novella "The Unknown Masterpiece." On the quay at the corner—the first embankment built in Paris—is the building that has housed the restaurant Lapérouse since the 1870s.

Behind the distinctive wood-paneled façade embellished with an elegant eighteenth-century iron balcony, these premises first housed a wine merchant, where wholesalers and retailers were able to strike their deals over a glass—the French equivalent of the English handshake—in the privacy of separate rooms. It is these fourteen salons that have given Lapérouse—named for a noted French navigator—its unique character as well as its early reputation as a discreet *rendez-vous* during an era when taking one's own wife to restaurants in the evenings was not done. Although the style of the individually decorated dining rooms mimics that of the French masters of the eighteenth century, the work actually dates to the 1880s when this kind of historical pastiche was an alternative to the reigning Art Nouveau. There is the *Salon des Anges* (angels), the *Salon des Singes* (monkeys), the *Salon des Glaces* (mirrors), and the *Salon de La Fontaine*, which features a portrait of the fabled fabulist.

Specialties at this restaurant that counts Victor Hugo, Guy de Maupassant, and Emile Zola among its former customers include *quenelles de brochet* (pike dumplings), turbot, Bresse chicken, and *pots de crème*, soufflés, and *pain perdu* (French toast) among the desserts. The food, however, is often criticized as not being worthy of the magnificent decor.

La Palette

43, RUE DE SEINE (6TH ARR.)
01.43.26.68.15
MÉTRO: MABILLON OR ST-GERMAIN
8AM-2AM; CLOSED SUNDAY & AUGUST

✦

A HUNDRED YEARS AGO, THE NOW CHIC AND EXPENSIVE SAINT-GERMAIN-DES-PRÉS was a terrible slum chosen by Emile Zola as the epitome of squalor in his novel *Thérèse Raquin*. This was a neighborhood of struggling artists living in unheated garrets who would join students from the nearby Ecole des Beaux-Arts at low-rent area cafés. La Palette, one of the few such cafés to have survived the area's profound transition, is at the center of this historic artistic quarter. Lovers Frédéric Chopin and George Sand had their portraits painted by their friend Eugène Delacroix around the corner in his *atelier* at 17, rue Visconti, where the young, unknown Claude Monet and Auguste Renoir later shared a studio at number 20. In 1902, an impoverished Pablo Picasso lived a true bohemian existence a few doors down from the café at 57, rue de Seine.

The casual La Palette is one of the best-loved cafés on the Left Bank, serving today's art students, local intellectuals, and tourists as well as dealers from the many small galleries that line the small, picturesque street. Customers stand, sometimes four and five deep, at the smoky front-room bar, which is adorned with the paint-encrusted palettes for which the café is named.

Among the historic cafés, La Palette is one of the few that has never enclosed its sidewalk *terrasse*, where in winter, old-fashioned braziers continue to warm Parisians loath to forfeit café-sitting on even the coldest, greyest days. Here, or at the simple wooden tables in the back room, *tartines* (French bread sliced lengthwise) with butter and jam or *croissants* are served for *petit-dejeuner*; salads, omelets (the *parmentier* is topped with sautéed potatoes), or *guillotines* (open-faced sandwiches on buttered Poilâne bread) are available at lunch. Evenings, La Palette is a good place to meet for drinks before or after dinner at one of the area's many restaurants.

Le Petit Saint-Benoît

4, RUE SAINT-BENOÎT (6TH ARR.)
01.42.60.27.92
MÉTRO: ST-GERMAIN
NOON-2:30PM & 7PM-10PM; CLOSED SUNDAY

✦

DESPITE THIS BISTRO'S LOCATION IN THE HEART OF FASHIONABLE SAINT-GERMAIN-des-Prés, its various proprietors have all resisted the impulse to gentrify the simple, time-worn premises. Once a canteen for horse-drawn-carriage drivers, this enduring one-hundred-and-forty-year-old still attracts a loyal following of both locals and tourists, who may wish to recoup some of the *francs* they have spent in the area's high-priced boutique hotels.

At the metal tables that have been set out on the narrow rue Saint-Benoît, or at the old brown-leather banquettes inside, diners are served simply prepared *hors d'oeuvres* such as the *assiette de crudités*, leeks *vinaigrette*, endive salad with *roquefort*, and *potage de legumes* (vegetable soup), and *plats du jour* such as *brandade de morue* (pureed salt cod and potatoes), *quenelles de brochet* (pike dumplings), *gigot d'agneau* (roast leg of lamb), and roast chicken. A warm *gratin* of clementines is a standout among the roster of typical *bistro* desserts such as *mousse au chocolat*, apple compote, and fruit *sorbets*.

The small zinc-topped bar, brass hat rack, and that vintage-*bistro* fixture, the old numbered napkin cabinet, complete the bare-bones decor.

Polidor

41, RUE MONSIEUR-LE-PRINCE (6TH ARR.)
01.43.26.95.34
MÉTRO: ODÉON
NOON-2:30PM & 7PM-11PM DAILY

✦

FOR CENTURIES, SMALL, AGILE GOATS WERE HERDED THROUGH THE CROWDED STREETS of Paris and up cramped, winding staircases to deliver milk-on-the-hoof to apartment dwellers. Eventually this service was replaced by *crémeries* that also offered cheeses, eggs, and butter. Polidor was one such dairy shop, opening in 1845 in the busy Odéon quarter. The area was known as the place where illiterate Parisians could find financially-strapped Latin Quarter scholars for hire as letter writers and readers. At the simple restaurant into which Polidor evolved in 1890, their descendants— working people and low-paid academics, eventually joined by tourists on a budget—have always been the chief clientele, dining through the decades literally elbow-to-elbow at the long wooden tables.

This is the genuine article, authentic and unrestored (down to the vexing antique *w.c.*). Vintage tin signs have probably hung in the same spot since they were new; an old *meuble à serviettes* (a wooden cabinet that held the napkins of regulars in numbered drawers until a hygiene law of 1948 outlawed their use) stands against the back wall beneath an array of variously sized champagne bottles. The place is almost always buzzing, with large groups engaged in lively conversation amid thick clouds of tobacco smoke. To keep the costs down and ensure a quick turnover, most of the specialties here are dishes that can be prepared ahead of time: *crudités*, cream of pumpkin soup, *boeuf bourguignon*, *blanquette de veau* (veal stew), roast chicken, *ragout de porc*, *tarte Tatin*, chocolate mousse, and *baba au rhum*.

Le Procope

13, RUE DE L'ANCIENNE-COMÉDIE (6TH ARR.)
01.40.46.79.00
MÉTRO: ODÉON
11AM–1AM DAILY

✦

ALEXANDRE DUMAS RECORDS THAT MADAME DE SÉVIGNÉ FOUGHT HARD AGAINST THE consumption of coffee following its introduction to France, and that she predicted that cafés were merely a novelty that would quickly pass out of fashion. Remarkably, among the thousands of French cafés that have come and gone in the three centuries since, Le Procope—credited with being the first—is one that remains.

Opened in 1686 during the reign of Louis XIV, on a street that would come to be named for the Comédie-Française, it was the theater's relocation there just three years later that ensured the café's success with performers and dramatists, Racine and Molière among them. A century later, its presence at the center of Left Bank revolutionary activity made it a favorite of the great political figures of the day. At that time, regulars made use of the *boules* lanes behind the rear façade in the newly opened passageway, the Cour du Commerce-Saint-André, where Dr. Louis Guillotin was working to perfect his new execution device on sheep. The "philanthropic decapitating machine" would soon claim the life of Charlotte Corday, whose infamous bathtub attack on Jean-Paul Marat took place in the victim's home just across what is now the boulevard Saint-Germain. (His ashes, along with those of Voltaire, were once actually enshrined at Le Procope.) Georges Jacques Danton, another café habitué who lived within the passage, would also be guillotined.

The much-enhanced red-and-gold "period" decor is complete with crystal chandeliers, gilt-framed mirrors, and portraits of Procope's celebrated customers. Despite its lengthy, colorful past, some dismiss today's establishment, now more restaurant than café, as little more than a stage-set replica of its former self, frequented primarily by tourists. Most of those dining there, however, appear to be fully enjoying themselves on such standards as duck *foie gras* with melon chutney, eggplant caviar, fresh shellfish platters, swordfish in puff pastry, duck *à l'orange*, *pot-au-feu*, grilled beef, and *coq-au-vin*.

Vagenende

142, BOULEVARD SAINT-GERMAIN (6TH ARR.)
01.43.26.68.18
MÉTRO: ODÉON
NOON-1AM DAILY

✦

OPENED AT THE TURN OF THE LAST CENTURY, VAGENENDE WAS PART OF A LARGE CHAIN of restaurants operated by the Chartier brothers, and is located only a few short blocks from their Latin Quarter property on the rue Racine (page 79). Taking over what had been a *pâtisserie* on this busy section of the boulevard Saint-Germain, the owners designed a restaurant that was much grander than those that usually catered to their middle-class clientele. Their high design standards are still evident in the three dozen small bucolic landscapes that were painted on glass and framed by the elaborate, curving Art Nouveau woodwork. At night, a sparkle of lights is multiplied in the succession of beveled mirrors in the large, deep dining room.

Although Vagenende provides a fairly formulaic dining experience, the lovely decor and its prime location on the liveliest part of the Left Bank's main thoroughfare ensure that the restaurant stays fairly crowded most evenings. Half a dozen types of fresh oysters and elaborate tiered presentations of shellfish are available from the raw bar outside, where several marble-topped café tables are available for seating. Other items on the menu include a spinach salad topped with chicken livers, *soupe de poissons*, *ratatouille*, *pétoncles* (small bay scallops) sautéed in olive oil and wine, grilled swordfish, *sole meunière*, and *pot-au-feu*. For dessert, Vagenende offers *clafoutis*, *baba au rhum*, and assorted *sorbets*.

SEVENTH

ARRONDISSEMENT

✦

Le Bistrot de Paris

33, RUE DE LILLE (7TH ARR.)
01.42.61.16.83
MÉTRO: BAC
NOON-2:30PM & 7PM-11:30PM DAILY

✦

LE BISTROT DE PARIS, A SHORT BLOCK FROM THE SEINE, IS A BRIGHT AND CONVIVIAL neighborhood restaurant that had already been in business for more than a decade when the nearby Gare d'Orsay opened in 1900. Today, the former train station houses the peerless national collection of French Impressionism and other nineteenth-century art, and the *bistro*'s proximity to the immensely popular museum has made it a favorite with foreign tourists, although some locals continue to patronize it as well. Newer decorative elements have been seamlessly added to the tastefully simple period interior of lace café curtains, bentwood chairs, old brass ceiling fixtures, and framed vintage advertising posters that have been combined in the cheerful, completely mirrored main dining room.

The restaurant's large menu relies heavily on Provençal dishes, including red peppers that are stuffed with avocado and smoked ham, artichokes that have been baked with goat cheese, tomato mousse with tarragon *sorbet*, tuna *carpaccio*, *rougets* (red mullets) *provençale*, roasted rabbit, roasted *lotte* (monkfish), and grilled beef with shallots. The apricot tart is the standout among the many desserts.

In fall and winter, Le Bistrot de Paris specializes in wild game.

Debauve & Gallais

30, RUE DES SAINT-PÈRES (7TH ARR.)
01.45.48.54.67
MÉTRO: ST-GERMAIN
10AM-1PM & 2PM-7PM
CLOSED SUNDAY & MONDAY

✦

WHEN BALZAC, PROUST, OR BAUDELAIRE WANTED CHOCOLATE, THEY WOULD HEAD for Debauve & Gallais, the Saint-Germain-des-Prés *confiserie* that was already a legend in their time. Modern visitors torn between their sweet tooths and their waistlines can only envy the nineteenth-century customers who shopped here at a time when products made from cocoa were deemed tonics for whatever ailed you. In fact, one of the founding partners had been a so-called "*pharmacien-chocolatier*" to no less than Louis XVI and Marie-Antoinette, whose favorite milk-chocolate-and-almond confection, *les pastilles de la reine*, was named in her honor. After the Revolution did away with those ill-fated royal patrons, Monsieur Debauve opened this retail shop and factory with his "chocolate-scholar" nephew, Gallais, bringing their healthful sweets to a wider, newly egalitarian clientele.

Now, unfortunately, equality has been set aside and only the most affluent Parisians can afford the wonders available in the pristine neoclassical setting. Amid faux-marble Corinthian columns, gilded mirrors, and large black-and-gold tole canisters, a magnificent semicircular carved oak counter displays the forty specialty chocolates that are presented in an atmosphere of hushed reverence usually associated with fine wine or jewelry shops. An antique brass-and-marble scale weighs the selected chocolate— some varieties delicately flavored with orange blossom, vanilla, coffee, jasmine, or Earl Grey (*bergamote*) tea, some filled with caramel, hazelnuts, or pistachios. *La boite maison 1800*, one of the boxed assortments, commemorates the year of the shop's founding.

Obviously, Debauve & Gallais' chocolates make impressive gifts to bring back home.

La Fontaine de Mars

129, RUE SAINT-DOMINIQUE (7TH ARR.)
01.47.05.46.44
MÉTRO: ÉCOLE MILITAIRE
NOON-2:45PM & 7:30PM-10:45PM DAILY

✦

THE EIFFEL TOWER WAS A CONTROVERSIAL RECENT ADDITION TO THE LOCAL LANDscape when this pretty little restaurant opened at the turn of the last century. Then a modest café, La Fontaine de Mars was named for the small nearby fountain depicting the god of war that had been commissioned in 1806 by Emperor Napoleon for a military hospital that existed on the site. The warm, welcoming restaurant has been consistently popular with residents of this *bien bourgeois* neighborhood to this day and can be crowded with regulars and newcomers even in the middle of the week.

With its lace curtains, moleskin banquettes, beveled mirrors, pink-and-white table linens, and tiny zinc-topped bar at the rear, the decor of La Fontaine de Mars is a traditional setting for its most traditional cuisine. Dinner might begin with such classics as *boudin noir* (pork blood sausage), *champignons à la grecque,* or leeks *vinaigrette.* The main courses that follow could include a *pot-au-feu,* *gigot d'agneau* (roast leg of lamb), *fricassée de canard* (duck stew), or *cassoulet de Toulouse*; among the desserts are plums in Armagnac and a vanilla-scented *crème brûlée* that is rated one of the best in Paris.

In good weather, several small tables are set out under the building's picturesque stone arcade.

La Pagode

57 BIS, RUE DE BABYLONE (7TH ARR.)
01.47.05.12.15
MÉTRO: ST-FRANÇOIS-XAVIER
4PM-10PM MONDAY-SATURDAY
2PM-10PM SUNDAY

✦

THE RAGE FOR ALL THINGS JAPANESE CAP-
TIVATED THE FRENCH IN THE MID-NINE-
teenth century as the exotic eastern empire emerged
from centuries of self-imposed isolation. From the
Impressionists, who were quick to reflect the influ-
ence of Japanese wood-block prints in their innova-
tive paintings, to fashionable *parisiennes*, who took
to accessorizing their crinolines with colorful
Japanese fans and parasols, it seemed as if the entire
city was caught up in the craze.

Perhaps the most extreme example of *japonisme*
in Paris, however, was the reconstruction of a genuine
pagoda by one of the executives of the fashionable
Bon Marché department store as a *folie* for his wife.
The temple was dismantled, carefully shipped to the
French capital, and reassembled in its new location
near the Hôtel des Invalides in 1895. The elaborate
carved wood structure, with its stained-glass windows,

and carved stone images of birds, dragons, lions, and buddhas made this a most unusual addition to the staid residential quarter that was characterized, like so much of the city, by street after street of nearly identical limestone buildings.

A century later, a palpable air of mystery surrounds the structure, which is set back from the street behind a tall wrought-iron fence, dense climbing vines, low-hanging tree branches, and a lily pond. After the property was converted in the 1930s into a cinema that featured a small *salon de thé* set in the ornamental Japanese garden, the pagoda became accessible to the public. Whether attending a film or visiting the nearby Musée Rodin, the unique ambience of the recently restored La Pagode provides a memorable setting for a late afternoon snack.

Poujauran

20, RUE JEAN-NICOT (7TH ARR.)
01.47.05.80.88
MÉTRO: LATOUR-MAUBOURG
8:30AM-8:30PM; CLOSED SUNDAY

✦

HISTORIC PRESERVATIONISTS AS WELL AS GOURMETS CAN CELEBRATE THE SUCCESS story that is Poujauran, a combination *boulangerie-pâtisserie* that twenty-five years ago took up residence in a dilapidated, abandoned nineteenth-century bakery. Its fanciful Belle Epoque interior was thereby rescued for an enterprise that would soon become an undisputed star in this most crowded and competitive Parisian field.

On a busy commercial street in a residential area of the Left Bank that is usually passed over by foreign tourists, the bright pink façade—reproduced on the lemon-yellow cardboard boxes—now entices a whole new generation of discriminating shoppers. Inside, the newly cleaned ceiling murals and restored etched mirrors are enjoying their second lease on life. Vintage brass-and-iron baker's racks display the house specialities: rustic *pain de campagne* (round country loaves), *seigle aux raisins* (rye

[113]

with raisins), and an organic *croissant biologique*, *brioches, ficelles*, and *pain de mie* (white sandwich bread) that the shop supplies to some of the finest restaurants in the city. From antique marble-topped counters, Poujauran also offers *financiers, tarte aux pommes rissolées* (almond custard tart studded with sautéed apple), *pains au chocolat, cannelés de Bordeaux* (bite-sized molded butter cakes), *quatre-quarts* (pound cake) as well as olive bread, sandwiches, *quiches,* and other savory tarts that can be carried a short distance to the esplanade in front of the Invalides or to the parc du Champs-de-Mars at the foot of the Eiffel Tower.

Restaurant Musée d'Orsay

1, RUE BELLECHASSE (7TH ARR.)
01.45.49.42.33
MÉTRO: SOLFÉRINO
11:30AM–2:30PM; THURSDAY UNTIL 9:30PM
CLOSED MONDAY

✦

WHILE IT IS NOT STRICTLY SPEAKING A HISTORIC RESTAURANT, THE DINING ROOM at the Musée d'Orsay is housed within historic premises, one of the grand Belle Epoque salons of the hotel that adjoined the former train station. Although less grand than the extravagant contemporaneous decor of Le Train Bleu—the restaurant at the Gare de Lyon (page 199)—here is a place where today's typically dressed-down museum visitors can comfortably lunch amid crystal chandeliers, marble fireplaces, enormous mirrors, parquet flooring, and an opulently gilded and frescoed ceiling.

A rarity in Paris is the all-you-can-eat, serve-yourself buffet and salad bar that provides *charcuterie, crudités*, and other prepared fare for those needing *restauration* after viewing the work of Monet, Renoir, van Gogh, and other masters of the period. *À la carte* offerings are described in several languages on the menu and include *soupe de poissons*, melon and smoked duck, pork in a mustard sauce, and grilled lamb or beef. Pale-green wicker arm chairs provide seating at the spaciously set tables.

Those taking the late afternoon *le goûter* Orsay can enjoy a selection from the heavily laden pastry cart with tea, hot chocolate, or several different coffees while listening to a pianist play selections from nineteenth-century composers.

Ryst-Dupeyron

79, RUE DU BAC (7TH ARR.)
01.45.48.80.93
MÉTRO: BAC
10AM-7:30PM
CLOSED SUNDAY & MONDAY MORNING

✦

ALTHOUGH IT IS NOT ONE OF THE GRANDER
THOROUGHFARES OF THE CITY, THE SIX-
teenth-century rue du Bac bears several minor dis-
tinctions. Named for a ferry service that transported
stones from a Left Bank quarry for the construction
of the now-vanished Tuileries Palace directly across
the river, the street was the birthplace of the
Barbizon painter Camille Corot, home to the expa-
triate American James McNeill Whistler, and the
location of the house where Chateaubriand lived the
last decade of his long life; Alexandre Dumas placed
the barracks for the dashing heroes of his 1844 *The
Three Musketeers* on the rue du Bac as well.

At the turn of the last century, a *liquoriste* specializing in Armagnac opened on the busy, narrow
street, a block from the intersection of the boulevard
Saint-Germain. In addition to having almost every
vintage Armagnac available since 1868, Ryst-

Dupeyron, whose stately carved-oak-and-glass façade has been listed as a historic monument, also stocks the grand wines of Bordeaux, as well as port, Calvados, Cognac, and champagne. Friendly and knowledgeable advice is offered and tastings are available at a large antique table. The shop is an excellent place to find gifts, with decanters, glassware, and related articles also offered for sale; for a small fee, the shop will prepare custom labels for bottles that can be given to commemorate a birthday, anniversary, or other special event.

Les Ambassadeurs

HÔTEL CRILLON
10, PLACE DE LA CONCORDE (8TH ARR.)
01.44.71.16.16
MÉTRO: CONCORDE
NOON-2:30PM & 7:30PM-10:30PM DAILY

✦

ONE OF THE MOST ARISTOCRATIC LUXURY RESTAURANTS IN PARIS COMMANDS A position overlooking the square whose name changes have alternately commemorated both the glory of the French aristocracy as well as its violent demise. The majestic eighteenth-century building that houses the palatial Hôtel Crillon has witnessed the dedication of the new *place* in 1757 to Louis XV; its use for the public execution of his grandson, Louis XVI, and Marie-Antoinette, when it was pointedly renamed place de la Révolution; and its ultimate rechristening as the conciliatory place de la Concorde in 1795.

The name of the current hotel restaurant, Les Ambassadeurs, refers to the proximity of several important embassies—the American is just across the street, the British around the corner—as well as to the famed *café-concert* of the same name that stood a stone's throw from here in the gardens of the Champs-Élysées. The stylish customers and bawdy entertainers of that Ambassadeurs were immortalized by Edgar Degas in several paintings.

Without question, the opulent dining room—once the palace's ballroom—is among the grandest and most romantic in Paris, embellished with *trompe l'oeil* paintings, and an extravagant use of many colored marbles, enormous crystal chandeliers that hang from the twenty-five-foot ceilings, and, atop the starched linen tablecloths, gold-plated cutlery, fine French china, and ornate silver candelabra. The modern *haute cuisine* served is also consistently rated among the most accomplished in the city, and features ravioli with duck *foie gras*, potato waffle with *brandade de morue* (pureed salt cod and potato) and Osetra caviar, roast turbot with tomato *confit* and thyme, pigeon roasted in cabbage leaves, crispy bass with almonds, fillet mignon of suckling pig, and medallions of lobster with caviar. Les Ambassadeurs is also singled out for the excellence of its coffee and cigar service.

The hotel also offers a regal tea service that can be taken in the lovely patio in warm weather.

Augé

116, BOULEVARD HAUSSMANN (8TH ARR.)
01.45.22.16.97
MÉTRO: ST-AUGUSTIN OR MIROMESNIL
9AM-7:30PM
CLOSED SUNDAY & MONDAY MORNING

✦

NOT FAR FROM THE STATUE OF BARON GEORGES-EUGÈNE HAUSSMANN ON THE boulevard that bears his name stands Augé, a *liquoriste* that first opened its doors in 1850, just a few years before Emperor Napoleon III entrusted Haussmann with the task of realizing his herculean plans to dismantle and reconfigure most of the city.

On the busy boulevard today, Augé's lovely antique façade, with its dark-wood-and-marble paneling, stands out amid the street's newer shops. Large plate glass windows contain artful arrangements of the abundant stock: fine wines, liqueurs, sherries, champagnes, Cognacs, Armagnacs, and *eaux-de-vie*, as well as quality glassware, crystal carafes, cut-glass decanters, and silver champagne buckets. A small brass bell attached to the old wooden door still announces the entry of customers into the dark and quiet shop. Tall shelves display row upon row of bottles and the aisles are crowded with open wooden crates that have been carefully stacked on the beautiful old tile floor.

The patient, knowledgeable staff will gladly assist with selections. Purchases are then paid for at the stunning carved-oak-and-glass cashier's desk.

Café Jacquemart-André

MUSÉE JACQUEMART-ANDRÉ
158, BOULEVARD HAUSSMANN (8TH ARR.)
01.42.89.04.91
MÉTRO: ST-PHILIPPE-DU-ROULE
OR MIROMESNIL
11:30AM-5PM DAILY

✦

LIKE THE ORNATE RESTAURANT AT THE MUSÉE D'ORSAY, THE CAFÉ AT THE JACQUEMART-André museum provides an opportunity for people not wishing to spend a fortune to dine in splendid historic surroundings for minimal expenditure. This small collection of fine Old Master paintings and sculpture housed in a mansion that was built for wealthy Parisian art collectors in 1875, however, draws a much different crowd than the much better-known Musée d'Orsay. Those slowly taking in the galleries or lunching in what was once the formal dining room tend to be older, more conservatively attired locals as well as foreigners.

Thanks to the fine eighteenth-century tapestries and Tiepolo ceiling painting that grace the carpeted, wood-paneled salon, this is one of the few no-smoking restaurants in Paris. The lunch specialties are composed salads that have been named for the esteemed artists in the museum's collection: the Mantegna (mixed greens with shrimp, chicken, grated carrots, and chopped peanuts); the Chardin (endive with *chèvre*, smoked ham, tomatoes, and nuts); and the Fragonard (spinach with smoked duck, *roquefort*, *haricots verts*, and cherry tomatoes). Following the lunch hour, an afternoon tea is served, and weekends a brunch is available. In good weather, there is additional seating on the terrace that overlooks the mansion's circular garden court.

No museum admission is necessary for entrance to the café.

Café Terminus

HÔTEL CONCORDE SAINT-LAZARE
108, RUE SAINT-LAZARE (8TH ARR.)
01.40.08.43.30
MÉTRO: ST-LAZARE
NOON-2:30PM & 7PM-10:30PM DAILY

✦

WHEN THEY TRAVELLED TO THE CAPITAL FROM THEIR HOME IN GIVERNY, CLAUDE Monet and his wife, Alice, would arrive in the artist's former Right Bank neighborhood at the Gare Saint-Lazare and take rooms at the facing railway hotel. The large Terminus Lazare had been built for the crowds anticipated at the Universal Exposition of 1889, in part by Gustave Eiffel, whose astounding tower was the fair's controversial centerpiece.

Today, the renamed Concorde Saint-Lazare's heavily restored restaurant features a rather generic hotel look: dark carpeting and wood paneling, beveled mirrors, and frosted-glass-and-brass chandeliers hanging from a low ceiling. And while it obviously draws many of its customers from among the hotel's visitors, it is also quite popular with business-suited Parisians from the area's many offices, shoppers from the nearby Galeries Lafayette and Le Printemps, and with suburban commuters headed to and from the busy station. For what the establishment lacks in ambience, it makes up for in the well-prepared fare offered on the large eclectic menu: several varieties of fresh oysters, vegetable *terrine*, duck *foie gras*, smoked salmon, lobster salad with *confit* of artichoke and peppers, *sole meunière*, calf's liver with raspberry vinegar, and guinea fowl in vine leaves with lemon and coriander. For dessert, there are assorted fruit tarts, *sorbets*, a *millefeuille* with berries and mascarpone, and *crêpes Suzette* flambéed with Grand Marnier.

99-101, RUE DU FAUBOURG-SAINT-HONORÉ
(8TH ARR.)
01.43.59.18.10
MÉTRO: ST-PHILIPPE-DU-ROULE
9AM-9PM DAILY; TEA ROOM: 8:30AM-7PM DAILY

✦

AT THE TIME OF ITS ESTABLISHMENT, THE
PREMISES THAT HOUSE THE PÂTISSERIE
Dalloyau lay outside the Paris city gates in the village of Roule, renowned for its fine goose market. Lined with elegant townhouses, the thoroughfare was the more aristocratic extension of the rue Saint-Honoré (named for the patron saint of pastry chefs) and was among those areas known as a *faubourg*, a "false borough," or suburb. Dalloyau predates by thirty-five years even Hermès, the luxury emporium that began its long life as a saddle maker several blocks east along the same street.

Today, the shop still sells pastries—fruit tarts, *éclairs*, and macaroons in a half-dozen flavors, and several varieties of chocolate cake, including the Mogador, layered with chocolate mousse and raspberry jam; the intensely rich Luxembourg (named for the location of one of five additional boutiques that overlooks those lovely Left Bank gardens); and an Opera cake that is still made according to a nineteenth-century recipe.

Over the years, Dalloyau has expanded its expertise into a respected catering service and to prepared foods, which are available to take away or to have on the spot in the sedate modern tea salon that is located upstairs above the shop.

Fauchon

26, PLACE DE LA MADELEINE (8TH ARR.)
01.47.42.60.11
MÉTRO: MADELEINE
9:40AM-7PM; CLOSED SUNDAY

✦

AUGUSTE FAUCHON WAS A MODERATELY SUCCESSFUL BUT HIGHLY AMBITIOUS greengrocer when he made his way from his native Normandy to the capital in 1886 at the age of thirty. He began with a simple pushcart among the flower vendors on the place de la Madeleine, where he soon opened one of several produce shops on the Right Bank. The one alongside the great neo-classical church has survived to become the most celebrated luxury food shop in Paris.

Now, more than three hundred and fifty employees tend Fauchon's three locations that are clustered around the northeast corner of the *place*. What the vast enterprise lacks in terms of the quality of the personal attention offered at smaller gourmet shops, it makes up for in terms of the epic quantity of the merchandise available. A *traiteur* offers all manner of prepared foods such as composed salads, smoked salmon, roasted chickens, *rata-*

touille, céleri rémoulade, a staggering display of fresh and aged cheeses—sheep's, goat's, and cow's milk—from France and the rest of Europe, crocks of *terrines*, truffles, *foie gras*, as well as scores of hams, sausages, and other *charcuterie*. In addition to the abundantly stocked *pâtisserie* and an *épicerie* with countless varieties of jams, mustards, spices, coffees, teas, and one of the best wine cellars in the city, Fauchon also offers a *salon de thé* as well as a restaurant, which was added in 1924.

In honor of the new century, some of Fauchon's packaging features vintage photographs of the shop's humble beginnings.

La Fermette Marbeuf 1900

5, RUE MARBEUF (8TH ARR.)
01.53.23.08.00
MÉTRO: ALMA-MARCEAU
NOON-3PM & 7PM-11:30PM DAILY

✦

IN 1978, CONSTRUCTION WORKERS WHO WERE EXPANDING A BANAL SELF-SERVICE restaurant on the rue Marbeuf off the Champs-Élysées were stunned as they removed a foot-thick plaster partition and uncovered a hidden Art Nouveau winter garden that had been all but forgotten for more than a generation.

Exactly eighty years after the new and stylish restaurant had first opened, its graceful cast-iron pillars, colorful ceramic tiles and stained glass, its sunflowers, peacocks, and dragonflies became visible once again. Skilled craftsmen were brought in to completely restore the interior of the small, gazebo-like dining room, and, by an extraordinary coincidence, a collection of identical vintage tiles from a private home outside Paris became available at auction. These were carefully removed, numbered, and reinstalled to outfit an entire second room for the restaurant; as a reward for their labors, the newly christened La Fermette Marbeuf 1900 was awarded classification as a historic monument.

The menu today features fillet of sole with basil, braised *ris-de-veau* (veal sweetbreads), *andouillette* (chitterlings sausage), roast saddle of lamb, mushroom *fricassée*, and a Grand Marnier soufflé.

Le Fouquet's

99, AVENUE DES CHAMPS-ÉLYSÉES (8TH ARR.)
01.47.23.70.60
MÉTRO: GEORGE V
BAR & CAFÉ: 9AM-2AM DAILY
RESTAURANT: NOON-3PM & 7PM-1AM DAILY

✦

THE MOST FAMOUS CAFÉ ON THE CHAMPS-ÉLYSÉES STARTED OUT AT THE TURN OF THE last century as a humble restaurant, with the owner cooking simple meals on a makeshift grill installed at the center of the dining room. As the year 1900 approached, all of Paris was preparing to greet hordes of visitors to the Universal Exposition, and a disemboweled Champs-Élysées was the site of the first line of the city's new underground train system, the *métropolitain.*

To ready his establishment at the corner of the avenue George V and set it apart from the competition, the enterprising Louis Fouquet followed the example of the hugely popular Maxim's (page 151), utilizing a non-French apostrophe, and promoting an anglicized pronunciation of his own surname. His instincts proved correct: from a canteen for the avenue's horse-drawn-carriage drivers, Fouquet's went on to become one of the most popular gathering spots for the city's fashionable carriage trade. Although its luster is somewhat diminished today, the place still draws a steady crowd, especially at the wide café terrace that overlooks one of the most animated sections of the newly refurbished Champs. For those interested in more than a drink, specialties include braised *ris-de-veau* (veal sweetbreads), *merlan au colbert* (fried whiting), and *hachis parmentier* (seasoned beef topped with mashed potatoes), as well as a selection from the highly-rated dessert cart.

Hédiard

21, PLACE DE LA MADELEINE (8TH ARR.)
01.42.66.44.36
MÉTRO: MADELEINE
9:15AM-7:30PM; CLOSED SUNDAY

✦

NINETEENTH-CENTURY SALESGIRLS IN FERDINAND HÉDIARD'S SMALL EMPORIUM on the place de la Madeleine found it necessary to instruct bewildered shoppers to discard the peel of its new exotic offering, the banana; their enterprising employer is also credited with introducing to France the mango, pineapple, guava, papaya, and other "colonial produce." Opened in 1854 at the beginning of Napoleon III's glittering Second Empire, Hédiard predates by more than three decades its now larger and more famous rival, Fauchon (page 131), on the opposite side of the church.

Despite a sleek new renovation that has created an inviting modern interior, the shop remains faithful to its founder's example, with rare and unusual delicacies still the stock and trade. Many Parisians cross the city to sample the scores of exceptional teas, coffees, chocolates, spices, jams, mustards, oils, and vinegars available alongside elegant prepared foods,

[137]

cheeses, *charcuterie*, pastries, delicate salad greens, aromatic fresh herbs, and, as always, flawless imported produce. Among its wines and spirits, Hédiard is considered to offer a superb selection of Bordeaux. A Provençal restaurant serves hungry shoppers on the second floor, offering no fewer than eight of the shop's many coffees.

Fleur de sel, the sea salt that is harvested on the Atlantic coast, the house-brand biscuits made with goat cheese and almonds, or the hot chocolate preparation are among the many items that make affordable, unbreakable gifts and souvenirs.

Ladurée

16, RUE ROYALE (8TH ARR.)
01.42.60.21.79
MÉTRO: MADELEINE
8:30AM-7PM DAILY

✦

WHEN ÉDOUARD MANET EXHIBITED HIS DARING "DÉJEUNER SUR L'HERBE" IN 1863, he scandalized the conservative *bourgeoisie* of the day. For the most part, the tastes of Second Empire Parisians ran to the soft and gauzy, epitomized by the reassuringly traditional rococo decor of the newly opened Ladurée, a *pâtisserie* and tea salon that featured gilded mirrors and plump, rosy-cheeked cherubs floating on a seafoam-green ceiling.

Many generations later, Ladurée, at the intersection of the rues Royale and Saint-Honoré, still caters to the affluent and conservative; the clientele is the predominantly soignée *dames d'un certain age* who have been shopping in the neighborhood's luxury boutiques. And despite the fact that diners are crowded together at the many small marble-topped tables, this remains a haven of nineteenth-century calm and civility a world apart from the modern city just outside the velvet-draped windows.

Although people do come in the mornings for a *café-crème* with the famed unglazed *croissants* (considered by many to be the best in Paris), the *brioches*, or *pains au chocolats*, Ladurée is most popular at lunch, with *bouchée à la reine* (puff pastry filled with creamed chicken), grilled steak, roast chicken, omelets, and a *salade composée* of *haricots verts*, sliced chicken breast, golden raisins, and hard-cooked egg dressed with a curry-seasoned *vinaigrette*. In late afternoon, delicate little tea sandwiches are paired with the beautifully fashioned house cakes, tarts, *éclairs*, macaroons, *petits-fours*, and chocolates.

From Ladurée, it is just a short walk across the pont de la Concorde to the Musée d'Orsay to visit Manet's "Déjeuner sur l'herbe."

Laurent

41, AVENUE GABRIEL (8TH ARR.)
01.42.25.00.39
MÉTRO: CHAMPS-ÉLYSÉES-CLEMENCEAU
NOON-2:30PM & 7:30PM-11PM
CLOSED SATURDAY LUNCH & SUNDAY

✦

AMONG THE MANY POWERFUL MEMORIES OF THINGS PAST THAT MARCEL PROUST WOULD transform into great literature was that of playing in the verdant gardens that border the lower section of the Champs-Élysées, where the writer has been honored with an *allée* that is named for him. Since Proust's time, the gardens—along with the several restaurants that then stood within them—have remained largely intact. Laurent, on the north side facing the avenue Gabriel, began its long life as a hunting lodge for Louis XIV when this part of Paris was still open countryside. In the early 1840s, Jakob Ignaz Hittorf, the architect who was responsible for the redesign of these gardens as well as the place de la Concorde where they begin, fashioned this site into a restaurant that would soon come to be named for one of its more esteemed managers.

Here, within the formal salons of the two-story

[141]

peach-and-cream neoclassical pavilion, or better yet, beneath the broad, leafy horse-chestnut trees in the lovely sheltered terrace, contemporary diners removed from the distractions of the modern city may still conjure a collective Proustian memory of that charmed former Paris.

Laurent, which is easily one of the most romantic restaurants in the city, offers high-priced classic *haute cuisine*, prepared with seasonal ingredients that vary according to the market. Among the notable dishes: salmon *carpaccio* with caviar, *langoustines* in pastry, roast lobster, veal chop, and that most elegant old-style dessert, *crêpes Suzette.*

Ledoyen

1, AVENUE DUTHUIT (8TH ARR.)
01.53.05.10.01
MÉTRO: CHAMPS-ÉLYSÉES-CLEMENCEAU
12:30PM-2:30PM & 8:30PM-10:30PM
CLOSED SATURDAY, SUNDAY & AUGUST

✦

AN EXPERT ON PARIS, AMERICAN HENRY JAMES INFORMED NINETEENTH-CENTURY travelers that they could dine at the restaurants in the gardens of the Champs-Élysées, "at a table spread under the trees, beside an ivied wall, and almost believe you are in the country." However, he warned, "This illusion, imperfect as it is, is a luxury and must be paid for accordingly."

Among those opulent havens, Ledoyen, today one of the city's oldest restaurants, was a *guinguette* (a rustic outdoor café) and dairy serving fresh milk when Louis XVI and Marie-Antoinette lost their heads to the guillotine in the nearby place de la Concorde. (Yet another victim of the blade, Robespierre, is reported to have enjoyed one of his last meals here just two days before his execution.) The owner, a Monsieur Doyen, sold the establishment in 1830, leaving only his name to the restaurant that was rebuilt on the premises in the next decade by Jakob Ignaz Hittorf, the architect whose building for Laurent (page 141) also figured in his master plan for these gardens.

Because of its location beside the old Palais de l'Industrie (replaced in 1900 by the Grand and Petit Palais), where each spring the powerful Salon displayed its annual selection of the best in painting and sculpture, the lavishly decorated Ledoyen became the place for well-heeled artists such as Édouard Manet and Edgar Degas to gather with friends and admirers for lunch on opening day.

More than a century later, James' advice still holds true, and the restaurant remains a bastion of the privileged few, who enjoy the roasted duck *foie gras*, *asparagus meunière*, *tête-de-veau*, *coquilles Saint-Jacques*, sautéed sole, and turbot with truffles in either the renowned garden or inside the landmarked upstairs rooms, amid fine beveled mirrors and floral murals.

Lucas-Carton

9, PLACE DE LA MADELEINE (8TH ARR.)
01.42.65.22.90
MÉTRO: MADELEINE
NOON-2:30PM & 8PM-10:15PM; CLOSED
SATURDAY LUNCH, SUNDAY & MONDAY LUNCH

✦

SINCE THE MIDDLE OF THE NINETEENTH CENTURY A RESTAURANT HAS EXISTED ON this enviable location, a corner site facing the majestic portico of the church of the Madeleine. On the premises today is Lucas-Carton, one of the most esteemed *haute-cuisine* restaurants in Paris. When compared to the opulent, kaleidoscopic decor at the contemporaneous Maxim's (page 151) and Le Grand Café Capucines (page 169) nearby, the understated Art Nouveau interior here, which was fashioned entirely from pale, blond woods and bronze, is memorable for its tasteful simplicity and sobriety.

Ironically, neither Monsieur Lucas nor Carton—who separately owned the establishment decades apart—was responsible for the sublime *fin-de-siècle* redesign that has earned the restaurant designation as a historic monument. In rooms adorned with highly polished, finely carved sycamore and maple paneling, expansive mirrored panels, tan uphol-stered banquettes, and fanciful female-headed bronze wall sconces, diners sample some of the most consistently touted cuisine in Paris: *foie gras* steamed in cabbage leaves, polenta with black truf-fles, ravioli filled with clams, red-mullet fillets with olives, lemon, and capers, frogs' legs and asparagus, and the house specialty, *canard Apicius* (duck that has been roasted with honey and spices). Bittersweet chocolate soufflé, and a *millefeuille* that is consid-ered to be one of the best in the city are among Lucas-Carton's desserts.

Maille

6, PLACE DE LA MADELEINE (8TH ARR.)
01.40.15.06.00
MÉTRO: MADELEINE
10AM-7PM; CLOSED SUNDAY

✦

THOMAS JEFFERSON, THE NEW AMERICAN REPUBLIC'S MINISTER TO FRANCE, WAS A regular customer of this venerable Dijon mustard purveyor. The spare and pristine Boutiques Maille that operates today on the place de la Madeleine, however, has been in business for just a few years, opening to commemorate the two-hundred-and-fiftieth anniversary of the company's 1747 founding.

Mustard has been an integral part of the French table since the Middle Ages, when *sauciers* (sauce-vendors) traveled through the streets at mealtime hawking their flavorful wares. It was not until the middle of the eighteenth century, however, that the condiment became fashionable with the aristocracy, when Monsieur Maille, a vinegar-distiller in service to the King, expanded his offerings by creating a series of mustards flavored with lemon, garlic, tarragon, nasturtium, truffles, and other exotic seasonings. Some of his original blends are still sold at the shop, along with many preparations that are not available elsewhere. With vinegars, *cornichons*, *eaux-de-vie*, and little faience mustard pots that are still hand-painted with the original designs, they make excellent, reasonably priced souvenirs and gifts. The shop also offers the unique service of pumping mustard to order into small, refillable crocks.

Printed cards provide recipes and suggestions for pairing particular foods with the perfect mustard: poultry and game with the Calvados, black currant, or raspberry mustard; red meats with cognac or blue cheese mustard; fish with champagne or *provençal* mustard; *charcuterie* with walnut or basil mustard.

Maison Faguais

30, RUE DE LA TRÉMOILLE (8TH ARR.)
01.47.20.80.91
MÉTRO: ALMA-MARCEAU OR FDR
9AM-7:30PM; CLOSED SUNDAY

✦

MARCEL PROUST'S FAMOUS CELEBRATION OF THE MADELEINE UNDOUBTEDLY WENT a long way toward ensuring the continued popularity of the humble little lemon-scented treat. Remembered far less often, however, is the tea into which he dipped his memory-provoking cake: *tilleul*, an infusion of lime blossoms from the linden tree. In Proust's day, one could purchase lime-blossom and other teas—black, green, herbal, and perfumed—at Maison Faguais, a charming establishment that has been in operation for close to a century near both of the writer's long-term addresses in the eighth *arrondissement*.

Customers here today can select from a large variety of both premium tea and coffee blends as well as *théières* (teapots), *cafetières* (coffee pots), canisters, cruets, and salt and pepper grinders. Maison Faguais also stocks tempting jams, honeys, mustards, chocolates, cookies, and crackers, all of which can be fashioned into impressive gift assortments that are arranged in attractive woven baskets or wooden boxes.

Maxim's

3, RUE ROYALE (8TH ARR.)
01.42.65.27.94
MÉTRO: CONCORDE
12:30PM-2PM & 7:30PM-MIDNIGHT
CLOSED SUNDAY

✦

FOR MANY DECADES, NO WELL-TO-DO TOURIST CONSIDERED A TRIP TO PARIS complete without a visit to Maxim's. The fabled night spot was the very model of the grand, florid Belle Epoque restaurant, the epitome of the see-and-be-seen destination. Gentlemen never dined here with their own wives, but came to show off their new mistresses; the *cocottes* came to Maxim's to show off their new jewels.

The restaurant's beginnings, however, were far less exalted. It was simply a mid-nineteenth-century *glacier* (ice cream parlor) near the place de la Concorde that was purchased in 1891 by one Maxime Gaillard, who left little to the premises other than his name. Only several owners later did the place—with the requisite flamboyant Art Nouveau interior of mahogany, copper, and colored glass—begin to acquire the great cachet that made it the most famous dining establishment in the city for years.

As Maxim's approached its centennial, informed opinion decried the over-restoration of the over-the-top decor, the mediocrity of the high-priced food, and the chill of the imperious service. Recently, however, a turnaround in the kitchen has brought favorable reviews for dishes that include Bresse chicken with tarragon sauce, sole on a bed of onions and artichokes, sea bass on a bed of radicchio, and rabbit roasted with rosemary.

Mollard

115, RUE SAINT-LAZARE (8TH ARR.)
01.43.87.50.22
MÉTRO: ST-LAZARE OR HAVRE-CAUMARTIN
DAILY UNTIL 1AM

✦

O F THE MANY ATTRACTIVE NEIGHBORHOODS OF PARIS, CLAUDE MONET AND ÉDOUARD Manet preferred the relatively colorless quarter around the Gare Saint-Lazare for their homes and studios. During the 1870s, they each even chose the busy train station itself as a worthy subject for their painting of modern Parisian life. In those years, a *bougnat* (a small primitive café) that principally sold coal and wood as well as various warming drinks, was operating across the rue Saint-Lazare from the depot. By 1895, its owners, a Monsieur and Madame Mollard, who had profited from the growing success of both the station and the large department stores that had recently opened nearby, decided to enlarge their establishment, redecorating it in the latest style, the Art Nouveau.

The resulting gold-and-pastel interior survives today as one of the most original in the city. Within the large dining rooms, with their variously colored marble columns, frosted-glass light fixtures, painted glass ceiling, and heavily carved woodwork, thousands of small multicolored mosaic tiles depict butterflies and dragonflies flitting among flowers and fruits. Additional tile murals illustrate the picturesque towns west of Paris that are reached by trains from the Gare Saint-Lazare. In one, a scene straight out of Manet, a young man in a straw boater rows a lady friend on the Seine.

At lunch, Mollard is full of people from area businesses; at night, however, it takes on a somewhat less spirited air. The extensive menu offers mussels, smoked salmon, *soupe à l'oignon*, *soupe de poissons*, grilled steak, *pommes allumettes*, steak *tartare*, *fricassée de poissons*, *Saint-Jacques provençales*, trout, *choucroute de la mer*, and lobster.

Le Pavillon Élysée

10, AVENUE DES CHAMPS-ÉLYSÉES (8TH ARR.)
01.42.65.85.10
MÉTRO: CHAMPS-ÉLYSÉES-CLEMENCEAU
NOON-2PM & 8PM-10PM
CLOSED SATURDAY & SUNDAY

✦

ONE OF THE GREATEST ACCOMPLISHMENTS OF NAPOLEON III'S GREAT REDESIGN OF Paris was the transformation of the gardens bordering the Champs-Élysées from a dangerous nest of murderers and thieves to the verdant, well-tended lawns we know today. The newly landscaped area quickly became dotted by glittering restaurants and festive *café-concerts*, merry-go-rounds, and puppet theaters, such as the 1818 Vrai Guignol, the city's oldest, which still stands in the gardens near the avenue Matignon.

By 1900, when the avenue had become the route along which the most fashionable Parisians promenaded in their fine horse-drawn carriages, a new restaurant constructed in the style of Louis XVI opened in the gardens near the avenue de Marigny. Today, the eclectic domed and turreted structure houses Le Pavillon Élysée, among the most exclusive and expensive gourmet establishments in town.

Like Laurent (page 141) and Ledoyen (page 143), Le Pavillon's privileged location provides an enviable garden terrace. The dining rooms feature a recent colonial-style decor, with wicker chairs, louvered shades, and potted palms beneath the building's original elaborately painted and stuccoed ceiling.

Among the starters: a salad of figs and fresh goat cheese dressed with balsamic vinegar; sardine filets with olive oil and basil. Main dishes include a lobster casserole or sautéed duck *foie gras* with rhubarb and raspberry vinegar. Pavillon Élysée serves a mousse of mascarpone and coffee ice cream or a *marbré* of apples and plums with fig *sorbet* among the dessert offerings.

Café de la Paix

12, BOULEVARD DES CAPUCINES (9TH ARR.)
01.42.68.12.13
MÉTRO: OPÉRA
10AM-1:30AM DAILY

✦

THERE WERE SEVERAL THOUSAND CAFÉS IN PARIS BY THE MIDDLE OF THE NINE-teenth century, with the largest and finest located on the central stretch of the famed *grands boulevards* between the Madeleine and the rue de Richelieu. The wide, tree-lined series of connecting avenues, which had been opened during the reign of Louis XIV on the old fortified bulwarks that once had pro-tected the city, were the undisputed center of fash-ionable Paris society. Stylish men and women would promenade here daily; even the omnibuses that worked the *grands boulevards* were pulled by three perfectly groomed white steeds.

Opening on the boulevard des Capucines in 1872, and soon the most cosmopolitan gathering spot in the city, was the Café de la Paix, which was housed in the new Grand Hôtel. From its prime location facing the sumptuous new gilded Opéra building, the café quickly attracted many notable regulars, including Guy de Maupassant and Emile Zola, the impassioned defender of the upstart Impressionist painters who, just two years later, held their first independent exhibition across the street at 35, boulevard des Capucines.

More than a century later, scores of customers still stop daily on one of the two long café terraces for a coffee, a glass of wine, a *coupe de champagne*, and some of the best people-watching in the city. Steak *tartare*, fresh shellfish, or *sole meunière*, among other fare is available there or in the café's handsome Second Empire interior dining area amid Corinthian columns, gilded moldings, and Italianate ceilings.

Chartier

7, RUE DU FAUBOURG-MONTMARTRE (9TH ARR.)
01.47.70.86.29
MÉTRO: GRANDS BOULEVARDS
11:30AM–3PM & 6PM–10PM DAILY

✦

DURING THE NINETEENTH CENTURY, ENTER-
PRISING BUTCHERS FREQUENTLY OPENED
soup counters in their shops, putting to good use the
scraps that remained at the end of the day. The most
successful of these soon evolved from sidelines to
primary businesses, a class of eatery that took the
name of the broth that was the mainstay of their
inexpensive fare. *Bouillons* eventually began catering to a more *bourgeois* clientele in large, extrava-
gantly decorated dining halls. A chain established by
the Chartier brothers, Camille and Edouard, opened
branches on both the Left and Right Banks during
the 1890s. Today, however, the location on the rue du
Faubourg-Montmartre is the only one to retain the
Chartier name and the only one to still offer aston-
ishingly low-priced meals.

Entering through a cobblestone courtyard, visitors
encounter a vast room with a narrow mezzanine-
level dining gallery. An enormous skylight to the

[161]

rear illuminates the communal tables that are separated by elaborate brass-and-carved-wood hat racks and coat stands. On the walls are beveled mirrors, marble wainscotting, wood paneling, vintage cabinetry that includes an old-style numbered napkin cupboard, and a bucolic landscape mural.

A fleet of middle-aged waiters clad in traditional long white aprons, black vests, and bow ties jot down orders on the paper that tops the pink-and-white table linens. Among the many simple offerings: *carottes rapées*, cucumber salad, *steak au poivre*, grilled lamb, roast chicken with *pommes frites*, sautéed brussels sprouts, *choucroute alsacienne*, peach compote, *coupe de crème chantilly*, chocolate mousse, *abricots melba*, and *parfait au caramel*.

Shortly after its hundredth anniversary, Chartier was listed as a historic monument.

Confiserie à l'Étoile d'Or

DENISE ACABO

30, RUE FONTAINE (9TH ARR.)

01.48.74.59.55

MÉTRO: BLANCHE

10:30AM-8PM

CLOSED SUNDAY & MONDAY MORNING

✦

THE LEGENDARY LE MOULIN ROUGE WAS STILL A NEW CABARET WHEN THIS LITTLE candy store opened down the street at the turn of the last century. Both Edgar Degas and Henri de Toulouse-Lautrec had recently lived on the rue Fontaine, one of several streets to the south of the place Pigalle and the *butte* Montmartre that were popular with artists. Very little has changed since then as Madame Acabo, the proprietor for the last three decades, has lovingly maintained the *confiserie's* original decor, its incomparable stock, and long-standing reputation.

From the old marble counter, the glass-fronted shelves, and a lace-draped antique table, she displays many traditional sweets whose recipes are even older than the shop itself: the finest hand-crafted candies from all over France. There are the bright orange-glazed almond *nougatines* from Nevers, made fashionable by Empress Eugénie after they were presented to her on her marriage in 1862; apple sugar from Normandy sold in long, cylindrical *batons*, a presentation conceived by a *confiseur* in Rouen in 1865 for Loulou, the *prince impérial*; and dark, caramelized-sugar-and-chocolate Négus, named in honor of the Ethiopian emperor and sold, as they have been since their invention in 1901, in beautiful black metal tins. Add to these *marrons glacés*, various fruit *confits*, and chocolates—with pistachio, mocha, almond, orange, and caramel, as well as the *jour et nuit* (day and night), a bar composed of both milk and dark chocolates

Fouquet

36, RUE LAFFITTE (9TH ARR.)
01.47.70.85.00
MÉTRO: LE PELETIER
9:30AM–7:30PM; CLOSED SUNDAY

✦

CLAUDE MONET, AN EPICURE AND TIRELESS ENTERTAINER AT HIS COUNTRY HOME AT Giverny, was never without a supply of the peerless bonbons from Fouquet, one of the premiere *confiseries* of the day. The shop had opened in 1852 on the very street where he had lived as a young boy near the church of Notre-Dame-de-Lorette.

Multicolored *berlingots*, almond *dragées*, *tablettes de chocolat* (chocolate bars), caramels, and many more of the nineteenth-century candies Monet knew and loved are still available at the handsome little shop, although the prices are undoubtedly far steeper than they once were. Still painstakingly prepared by hand to the original recipes, these can be purchased by weight, and packaged in an assortment of exquisitely colored tins to make excellent, easily transportable gifts. Other sweets include a variety of honeys and jams, and whole fruits, such as apricots, plums, and cherries immersed in syrup or *eaux-de-vie* in little glass jars with Fouquet's distinctive chocolate-brown lids. Also available are savory products such as *cornichons*, tinned *béarnaise* and other sauces, many flavored mustards, olive oils, and vinegars, as well as dried herbs, sea-salt and peppercorn mixtures.

Fouquet—not to be confused with the celebrated café on the Champs-Élysées (page 135)—has maintained a "new" shop on the rue François 1er in the eighth *arrondissement* since the 1920s.

Au Général La Fayette

52, RUE LA FAYETTE (9TH ARR.)
01.47.70.59.08
MÉTRO: LE PELETIER OR CADET
10AM-4AM DAILY

✦

I N THE NINETEENTH CENTURY, MOST PARISIANS FOR WHOM WINE WAS AS NECESSARY to life as water—viewed beer consumption as lowly, ignoble, and, above all, foreign. Some egalitarian entrepreneurs, however, embraced the minority beer-drinking population that was primarily made up of French provincials and tourists—Germans, Belgians, and Britons—and opened eateries designed to serve them.

Distinct from the city's many beer-centered Alsatian *brasseries*, Au Général La Fayette is something more unusual, a convivial Parisian tavern. Operating since 1886 on a busy corner near the *grands boulevards* and the Folies-Bergère, it boasts a dozen draft beers drawn from beautiful gleaming brass pumps and scores of imported and domestic bottled beers and ales that are served at the bar or in the spacious paneled dining room. The simple, well-prepared meals include a variety of omelets, *salades composées, saucisson de Lyon* (garlic-flavored pork sausage) with *pommes frites*, and platters of cheese, *charcuterie*, or smoked fish. Desserts such as *crème caramel*, chocolate mousse, a pastry of the day, and ice creams complete the meal.

Although this part of the ninth *arrondissement* is primarily a business district, the General La Fayette typically remains active well past midnight.

Le Grand Café Capucines

4, BOULEVARD DES CAPUCINES (9TH ARR.)
01.43.12.19.00
MÉTRO: OPÉRA
OPEN 24 HOURS DAILY

✦

DESPITE ITS INTERNATIONAL NOTORIETY AS THE CITY OF DAZZLING, RISQUÉ NIGHTLIFE, a century ago most of Paris actually went to bed quite early. The great exceptions, however, could be found up in Montmartre, with its bawdy music halls, and along the *grands boulevards*, with their glittering large cafés. Among those, the centrally located Grand Café Capucines was one of the very few that stayed open throughout the night—as it still does—its glowing plate glass windows a beacon to revelers returning from late parties, the many theaters of the neighborhood, or from the palatial Opéra building located just around the corner.

Although the dizzying Belle Epoque interior undoubtedly suited those boisterous nocturnal celebrants, modern sensibilities might deem the stained-glass ceilings, painted tile murals, and exotic statuary as a bit over the top. And while it is probably not the destination of many French gourmets, the place draws a steady clientele looking for a quick meal, day or night, in cheerful surroundings. The standard menu includes platters of fresh oysters, shellfish assortments, onion soup, grilled meats, and grilled, poached, or sautéed fish. Elaborate desserts include a raspberry soufflé, the *gourmandise de l'opéra* (*crème brûlée* and *profiteroles*), and *la vie en rose* (raspberry, strawberry, and sour-cherry *sorbet* with a strawberry *coulis*).

The Grand Café Capucines, itself, became a part of history on December 28, 1895, when three-dozen customers paid a *franc* each to witness the Lumière brothers' first public cinematic performance in the so-called *salon indien* downstairs.

À La Grange Batelière

16, RUE DE LA GRANGE-BATELIÈRE (9TH ARR.)
01.47.70.85.15
MÉTRO: RICHELIEU-DROUOT
12:15PM-2:30PM & 7:30PM-10:30PM
CLOSED SUNDAY

✦

THE RUE DROUOT JUST NORTH OF THE GRANDS BOULEVARDS HAS BEEN HOME TO the principal fine arts auction house in Paris since 1860, and the immediate area has long been the city's premier gallery district. In 1876, the renegade Impressionist painters who could not find acceptance at the government-sponsored Salon organized a second independent exhibition of their works in the heart of the neighborhood on the rue Le Peletier, where they were received with violent criticism and derision. That same year, a modest restaurant opened around the corner on the rue de la Grange-Batelière, a restaurant that still attracts art dealers, auction buyers, and others doing business in the quarter among its regular clientele.

Today, the interior of the welcoming little *bistro* features a floor that is a crazy-quilt arrangement of several surviving tile designs and a large marble-topped bar that conceals a steep and narrow staircase leading to the basement. The printed menu is decorated with a charming vintage butter advertisement; more antique posters and the original numbered napkin rack adorn the simple pink walls. Artichoke raviolis, chilled tomato soup with basil, marinated herring, and pimientos stuffed with eggplant caviar are among the available starters. Main courses include sautéed *rougets* (red mullets), *espadon* (swordfish) in a vinegar-based sauce, and caramelized roast pork. A cheese plate, melon soup, or *tiramisù* with berries complete the meal.

In season, La Grange Batelière specializes in deer, partridge, and other wild game.

La Maison du Miel

24, RUE VIGNON (9TH ARR.)
01.47.42.26.70
MÉTRO: MADELEINE OR HAVRE-CAUMARTIN
9:30AM-6PM MONDAY
9:30AM-7PM TUESDAY-SATURDAY
CLOSED SUNDAY

✦

THERE IS A MARKED CONTRAST BETWEEN THE SWEETNESS OF THE PRINCIPAL PRODUCT and the seriousness of its sale at the turn-of-the-century honey emporium where stylized Art Nouveau bees decorate the façade and the floor tiles. Lest one think that eating honey were merely a guilty pleasure, brochures detail the purported health benefits of the many varieties from the Auvergne, Corsica, the Alps, and the Vosges mountains—rosemary, thyme, acacia, eucalyptus, sunflower—and the nutrient-rich *gelée royale*, produced by the colony for feeding the queen. Honey also finds its way into an array of beauty products—soaps, shampoos, face masks, and even toothpaste—as well as into various honey-sweetened candies, cookies, and *pain d'épice*, the sticky gingerbread that is traditionally eaten by French schoolchildren at

Easter, New Year's, and other holidays.

La Maison du Miel, located since 1898 on a commercial side street near Hédiard (page 137), Fauchon (page 131), and the other historic gourmet shops that have always clustered around the church of the Madeleine, also sells beeswax candles and provides recipes for preparing all sorts of dishes with their honeys: asparagus mousse with clover honey, leg of lamb with wildflower honey, duck with linden-tree honey, *sorbet au miel* with lavender honey from Provence, and *crêpes* with pineapple, orange, rum, and chestnut honey.

À la Mère de Famille

✦

WITH FEW CONCESSIONS TO THE MODERN AGE, THIS WONDROUS TIME-CAPSULE COMbination *confiserie/épicerie* has catered to the residents of this Right Bank quarter since the middle of the eighteenth century, a hundred years before either the Folies-Bergère or the Musée Grévin (the Paris wax museum) opened nearby. Tinned violets from Toulouse and the distinctive elongated boxes of *calissons d'Aix*, the famed glazed-marzipan biscuits that have been made in Provence since 1854, are arranged on antique wooden cabinets with old enamel fittings.

Wicker baskets and vintage glass apothecary jars are stocked with dried and candied fruits—*marrons glacés* (candied chestnuts), *pruneaux d'Agen* (dried plums from southwestern France)—as well as all manner of bonbons, spice breads, cookies, and crackers. Mirrored shelves display colorful bottled liqueurs, artisanal *confitures*, honeys, and *pâtés*.

A refrigerated case offers dozens of fine caramels and chocolates sold by weight, including the *délices de la mère de famille* (marzipan studded with raisins that have been macerated in rum and then dipped in milk chocolate) that are still made by hand on the premises. Open burlap sacks brimming with dried nuts sit out on the star-patterned tile floor that long ago was emblazoned with the shop's quaint name. One pays for purchases at the old-fashioned glassed-in wooden cashier's booth.

Au Petit Riche

25, RUE LE PELETIER (9TH ARR.)
01.47.70.68.68
MÉTRO: RICHELIEU-DROUOT OR LE PELETIER
NOON-2:15PM & 7PM-12:15AM
CLOSED SUNDAY

✦

EDGAR DEGAS BEGAN HIS FAMOUS PAINT-INGS AND SCULPTURES OF YOUNG DANCERS not at the Palais Garnier, where ballet has been performed since 1875, but at the old Paris opera house that stood a few blocks to the east until it was destroyed by a fire two years earlier. Almost all the buildings in the rue le Peletier fell victim to that day-long inferno, including Au Petit Riche, a simple *bistro* at the corner of the rue Rossini that had been an informal canteen to the backstage workmen of the opera since 1854. (While this "little" Riche welcomed these "little people," its namesake, the far more elegant Café Riche, down the street at the boulevard des Italiens, catered to the composers and performers as well as to wealthy businessmen and politicians.)

After the fire, the restaurant's owner decided to rebuild, his new 1880 façade and interior decor surviving essentially intact until today. Beyond the paneled oval foyer, a series of lovely small dining salons features upholstered banquettes, vintage brass hat racks, frescoed ceilings, tiled floors, and tall mirrors etched with brimming fruit bowls and cornucopias.

The foods and wine of the Touraine are the specialty for modern customers—well-heeled business people by day, theater-goers at night. In addition to fresh seafood platters, *hors d'oeuvres* include a lentil salad, duck *terrine* with pistachios, and salmon marinated in black-truffle juice. *Sole meunière*, haddock, as well as roast lamb, grilled steak, *blanquette de volaille* (chicken stew), and *tête de veau* comprise the main-course listings. Au Petit Riche offers the usual *bistro*-style desserts and, unusually, a *prix-fixe* children's menu.

Restaurant Opéra

GRAND HÔTEL INTER-CONTINENTAL
5, PLACE DE L'OPÉRA (9TH ARR.)
01.40.07.30.10
MÉTRO: OPÉRA
NOON-2PM & 7:30PM-10:30PM
CLOSED SATURDAY & SUNDAY

✦

WHEN THE EXALTED EMPRESS EUGÉNIE OFFICIALLY INAUGURATED THE BALLROOM of the enormous new Grand Hôtel in 1863, she pronounced the palatially outfitted edifice "exactly like home." The glittering decor awed most contemporary Parisians, although an appalled Charles Baudelaire decried the hotel's lavish dining room, where he believed "all history and mythology were exploited in the service of gluttony."

Today, the exclusive, top-rated restaurant, which faces the gleaming, newly restored Opéra Garnier, is still opulent even by Paris standards, with gilded Corinthian columns, a rococo-style painted ceiling, and towering exotic floral displays. The menu features modern-day interpretations of classic French *haute cuisine*: *foie gras de canard* with rhubarb *confit*, potatoes and Osetra caviar, sole in mushroom sauce, roast turbot with *celeri rémoulade* and green peppercorns, pigeon breast with zucchini, asparagus tips, and tomato. The beautifully presented desserts include roast pineapple with aged rum, cinnamon-scented roasted figs, and a *millefeuille* with apple confit, Calvados, and green-apple *sorbet*.

TENTH

ARRONDISSEMENT

✦

Brasserie Flo

7, COUR DES PETITES-ÉCURIES (10TH ARR.)
(ENTER AT 63, RUE DU FAUBOURG-ST-DENIS)
01.47.70.13.59
MÉTRO: CHÂTEAU D'EAU
NOON-3PM & 7PM-1:30AM DAILY

✦

DESPITE THE FACT THAT MOST PARIS BRASSERIES WERE OWNED BY REFUGEES who fled from Alsace-Lorraine after France lost the province in the Franco-Prussian war, these and other businesses with Germanic names were often vandalized during the increasingly tense years leading up to the First World War. Following the near destruction of Hans, an 1886 ale house in a cobble-stone mews off the rue du Faubourg-Saint-Denis, the cautious owner, a Monsieur Floderer, rechristened his restaurant using the more neutral-sounding abbreviation of his last name. Happily for modern lovers of whimsical vintage decor, he kept the *brasserie*'s charming Bavarian interior.

In contrast to the more typical French Art Nouveau of Bofinger (page 55) and Julien (page 185) just down the street, the front room of Flo features a low coffered ceiling, richly colored leaded-glass windows, and dark leather seating. On the walls, inlaid wood paneling and mural paintings of jolly, beer-drinking gnomes complete the look of a warm, welcoming tavern. Luminous landscapes of Alpine lakes dominate the lighter back room, where an antique nickelodeon stands among the tables.

Because of its out-of-the-way location, no one stumbles onto Flo. This restaurant has survived on the strength of generations of loyal customers— Sarah Bernhardt was an early regular—and newcomers who have been encouraged to make the effort. All are rewarded with a traditional *brasserie* cuisine featuring a variety of fresh oysters and other crustaceans from the raw bar out front and the various brimming *choucroute* platters, *foie gras*, salmon *tartare* seasoned with chives, onions, and peppercorns, and roast veal with morels. The *coupe Flo*, cherry ice cream with cherry *eau-de-vie*, is among the house desserts.

16, RUE DU FAUBOURG-SAINT-DENIS
(10TH ARR.)
01.47.70.12.06
MÉTRO: STRASBOURG-ST-DENIS
NOON-3PM & 7PM-1:30AM DAILY

✦

ALTHOUGH THE DEATH OF THE ORIGINAL OWNER DELAYED THE OPENING THAT WAS scheduled to coincide with the 1889 Universal Exposition, this *brasserie* near Louis XIV's triumphal arch on the boulevard Saint-Denis has more than made up for lost time, enduring long enough to be listed today as a national historic monument. Even in Paris, there are few places that can match the splendor of Julien's dazzling Art Nouveau interior, a feature that attracts large convivial groups of locals and foreign tourists who would be too conspicuous in the city's smaller, more formal restaurants.

Then as now, customers sit on vintage Thonet-designed chairs or red-velour banquettes beneath large stained-glass ceiling panels and globe lights that are reflected in the succession of beveled mirrors. The most memorable features at Julien, however, must be the magnificent zinc-topped mahogany bar and the lovely maidens personifying the four seasons created by a popular *fin-de-siècle* technique of painting on glass. These and other *pâte-de-verre* panels featuring poppies, geraniums, lilies, and two majestic peacocks silhouetted against an opalescent full moon and shimmering stars are all set within sinuous high-relief stucco moldings.

Smoked salmon blinis, fish soup, *escargots*, sliced *foie gras* with lentils, platters of fresh raw oysters, or white asparagus in season might be followed by goose *cassoulet, sole meunière*, lobster, or chicken with morels. Desserts include *profiteroles* drizzled with hot chocolate sauce, a *charlotte* of pears and gingerbread, or green-apple *sorbet* splashed with Calvados.

Restaurant de la Grille

80, RUE DU FAUBOURG-POISSONNIÈRE
(10TH ARR.)
01.47.70.89.73
MÉTRO: POISSONNIÈRE
NOON-2:30PM & 7:15PM-10PM
CLOSED SATURDAY & SUNDAY

✦

OF ALL THE OLDER RESTAURANTS IN PARIS, THE RESTAURANT DE LA GRILLE MOST resembles a cozy, cluttered nineteenth-century parlor. Freshly pressed white lace and damask dominates the small crowded dining room with its embossed deep-red walls, frieze of oval mirrors, and pots of dried hydrangeas. Here, in a space that barely seats two dozen people, nearly a hundred vintage *chapeaux* from the owner's amusing collection are displayed on the overhead brass hat racks.

The current restaurant is only about thirty years old, having taken up in the premises of a nineteenth-century cabaret and wine shop that served northern coastal fishermen whose horse-drawn carts brought their catch into the wholesale market at Les Halles along the rue du Faubourg-Poissonnière (a *poissonnière* is a fishwife). Much of

La Grille's menu pays homage to the street's history, including herring filets, seafood *terrine*, grilled turbot with *beurre blanc*, and *brochette de Saint-Jacques* (skewered sea scallops); for carnivores, there's a rough-hewn *andouillette* (chitterlings sausage), *tête-de-veau*, a *boeuf bourguignon*, and steak with a butter-and-shallot sauce.

The relaxed and friendly establishment takes its name from the landmarked, two-hundred-year-old iron grillwork on the building's façade, whose bunches of grapes and head of Bacchus once advertised the original shop's inventory; today the god of wine has given his name to the owner's large dog.

ELEVENTH

ARRONDISSEMENT

✦

Le Bistrot du Peintre

116, AVENUE LEDRU-ROLLIN (11TH ARR.)
01.47.00.34.49
MÉTRO: LEDRU-ROLLIN
8AM–2AM DAILY

✦

DESPITE THE GRAND-SCALE GENTRIFICA-
TION AT THE END OF THE TWENTIETH
century, the Bastille quarter is still home to furniture
makers and other artisans who have been active in
this eastern working-class *arrondissement* for several
hundred years. Some of the neighborhood cafés and
bistros that traditionally catered to them have managed to remain in business, among them Le Bistrot
du Peintre, which occupies a shallow corner site
where two of the district's main thoroughfares
intersect. Like a poor man's Lucas-Carton (page
145), this Art Nouveau gem is as exuberant in design
as it is subdued in color. The low-key, friendly café
boasts an almost uniformly beige/brown interior
embellished with a long, curving, zinc-topped bar,
comfortable high-back caned barstools, biomorphic-
shaped mirrors, sinuous woodwork and plasterwork,
and a beautiful spiral staircase that leads to the
quieter second-floor dining-room.

The classic café/*bistro* fare, which is also available on the attractive sidewalk terrace, includes a salad of endive with *roquefort* and nuts, a traditional onion soup, shredded carrots dressed with lemon juice, *entrecôte* with herbed butter, *andouillette* (chitterlings sausage) in a mustard-and-cream sauce, *gratin* of macaroni and ham, *charcuterie* plates, cheese plates, and for dessert, *clafoutis*, assorted tarts, and a large selection of ice creams and *sorbets* from the celebrated Berthillon on the Ile-Saint-Louis.

Le Chardenoux

1, RUE JULES VALLÈS (11TH ARR.)
01.43.71.49.52
MÉTRO: CHARONNE
NOON-2:30PM & 8PM-10:30PM
CLOSED SATURDAY LUNCH & SUNDAY

✦

MORE THAN A DOZEN SEGMENTS OF VARI-OUSLY-COLORED MARBLES COMPRISE THE front of the curving zinc-topped bar at Le Chardenoux, making it one of the most beautiful in Paris. In fact, the restaurant's original owner was so proud of his *comptoir* that he named his establishment after a brand of French soap that was specifically formulated to scrub zinc surfaces. The bar, along with the delicately etched glass partition that separates the two parts of the L-shaped dining room, the ethereal Art Nouveau frescoes, and the exuberant stucco moldings make this working-class corner *bistro* one of the best-preserved turn-of-the-century interiors in the city.

Although Chardenoux is located in a quiet backwater ten blocks east of the busy place de la Bastille, the restaurant is full most nights. Diners may begin a meal with a *cardinal*, an intensely-colored crimson *kir* made with red wine instead of the usual white burgundy. Among the starters on the menu: endive salad, a creamy lentil-and-garlic soup, *foie gras*, rabbit *terrine*, *haricots verts*, and leeks in a beet *vinaigrette*. For the main course: veal with morels, roast lamb with thyme, veal kidneys, *magret de canard*, cod *à la florentine*, *lotte* (monkfish) in a saffron broth, grilled salmon, and two different preparations of tripe. Dessert choices include *crème caramel*, *sorbets*, vanilla ice cream with a hot caramel sauce, *mousse au chocolat*, raspberry cake, and *omelette norvégienne*, a light-as-air meringue preparation.

ARRONDISSEMENT

✦

Jacques Bazin

85 BIS, RUE DE CHARENTON (12TH ARR.)
01.43.07.75.21
MÉTRO: LEDRU-ROLLIN OR REUILLY-DIDEROT
7:30AM-8:30PM
CLOSED WEDNESDAY & THURSDAY

✦

INVOKING THE CONVENTIONAL WISDOM OF HIS DAY, ALEXANDRE DUMAS CONTENDED IN his celebrated nineteenth-century treatise on food that the generally robust health of the French people could be attributed to their relatively high rate of bread consumption. This sustained national devotion to eating bread also undoubtedly accounts for the remarkable proportion of neighborhood *boulangeries* among the nineteenth-century shops that have survived in twenty-first-century Paris.

Jacques Bazin, in the twelfth *arrondissement*, a short stroll from the bustling place de la Bastille, is one such bakery—a small wedge-shaped corner shop whose owners have managed to keep its original painted mirrors, faience tiles, and decorative plasterwork in beautiful condition for the past hundred years. Area residents often form lines that extend out the door, patiently waiting to purchase *baguettes*, *ficelles*, and other breads that can be found in most French bake shops as well as some distinctive, less typical loaves such as the house specialty, *pain bûcheron* (woodcutters bread), which is made with whole-wheat flour, rye flour, and sunflower seeds. Bazin also produces a large selection of organic breads.

Le Train Bleu

GARE DE LYON
20, BOULEVARD DIDEROT (12TH ARR.)
01.43.43.09.06
MÉTRO: GARE-DE-LYON
NOON-1:45PM & 7PM-10PM DAILY

✦

NO DESCRIPTION OF THE RESTAURANT AT THE GARE DE LYON WILL FAIL TO USE THE words sumptuous, ornate, opulent. Not a single square inch in this suite of enormous rooms—which narrowly escaped demolition during the "*moderne*" 1950s—is lacking in some manner of ornament, embellishment, or flourish.

Incongruously poised on the mezzanine above the station's drab platforms and tracks are dozens of frosted-glass sconces, crystal chandeliers, towering exotic floral displays, high-relief gilded stuccowork, and sensuous allegorical statues. Set within this extravagant framework are the luminous, thirty-six-foot-high paintings that the enterprising directors of the railway commissioned of the sunny Riviera towns to which their fabled southbound "Blue Train" conveyed travelers: Nice, Monaco, Antibes, Orange, and Marseilles. Additional murals depict

[199]

Paris landmarks such as the Institut de France, Notre-Dame cathedral, and the Pont Alexandre III, the rococo bridge across the Seine that, like the Gare de Lyon itself, was constructed for the Universal Exposition of 1900.

Amid this epic splendor, more than one hundred diners can be accommodated on the wood-framed, brown-leather banquettes—outfitted with generous overhead brass luggage racks that befit a grand train-station restaurant. Departing and arriving travelers, large families out for a celebration, and tourists lunch or dine on rack of lamb, *côte de veau*, roast duck with peaches, *provençal* beef stew, *quenelles de brochet* (pike dumplings), Lyonnaise sausages, and other specialities of the South of France. Many people, however, prefer to forego a full meal and enjoy the same palatial decor from one of the low club chairs for the price of a drink or afternoon tea.

THIRTEENTH
ARRONDISSEMENT

✦

Le Petit Marguery

9, BOULEVARD DU PORT-ROYAL (13TH ARR.)

01.43.31.58.59

MÉTRO: LES GOBELINS

NOON-2PM & 7:30PM-10PM

CLOSED SUNDAY, MONDAY & AUGUST

✦

IN THE THIRTEENTH ARRONDISSEMENT, A LITTLE-VISITED LEFT BANK NEIGHBORHOOD known primarily for the historic, still-active Gobelins tapestry works, is the last remaining outpost of a once-thriving chain of *fin-de-siècle bistros*, Le Petit Marguery. On the glass-enclosed terrace and in several comfortable adjoining dining rooms the past has been neither obliterated nor enshrined. The old chandeliers and patterned tile floors remain, but the mirrored walls have been updated with several shades of warm rose-toned paint.

Traditionally attired waiters carefully advise diners on the restaurant's extensive *prix-fixe* menu—a choice of either a starter and main course or a main course and dessert—that specializes in wild duck, pheasant, partridge, boar, and other game (*gibier*) in season. The list of available dishes changes frequently depending on what is freshest in the market, but appetizers may include a *terrine* of sea scallops with *fines herbes*, green lentil salad, and *escargots de bourgogne* (snails with garlic, butter, and parsley), and the main dishes may include skate roasted with coarse-grained mustard, haddock with cabbage, pigeon or guinea-fowl with *cèpes* mushrooms. A *gratin* of pear with gingerbread, orange *sorbet* with vodka, and cherries in *eau-de-vie* are among the many dessert options.

FOURTEENTH
ARRONDISSEMENT

LE PAVILLON MONTSOURIS · 207

✦

20, RUE GAZAN (14TH ARR.)
01.45.88.38.52
MÉTRO: CITÉ UNIVERSITAIRE
DAILY UNTIL 10:30PM

✦

ALONG WITH THE BOIS DE BOULOGNE IN THE WEST AND THE BOIS DE VINCENNES IN the east, the Parc Montsouris in the south of Paris is one of Napoleon III and Baron Haussmann's most significant contributions to a city that before 1850 offered a scant forty-seven acres of public greenery to its citizens. From deep in the fourteenth *arrondissement*, an army of landscapers labored for more than a decade to transform several abandoned stone quarries into one of the loveliest and least-frequented open spaces in the city. Set among the newly planted trees, shrubs, and lawns of the artful, artificially hilly terrain were a man-made lake—with a small island picturesquely populated by swans—serpentine paths, carriage roads, and, finally, a sizeable dining pavillon that was located on the eastern edge of the park.

Obviously, the Pavillon Montsouris, which is popular with large family groups out to celebrate birthdays, anniversaries, and other special occasions, is best visited in fine weather when seating is available under the leafy canopies of the now-mature specimen trees. Here, or inside the restaurant's greenhouse-like dining room, which is decorated in frilly pastel hues, breakfast and afternoon tea are both served in addition to lunch, weekend brunch, and dinner. The menu features *soupe de poissons provençale*, *cabillaud rôti* (roast codfish), wild duck, roast hare, *tête-de-veau*, and a pear *millefeuille*.

ARRONDISSEMENT

✦

Je Thé...me

4, RUE D'ALLERAY (15TH ARR.)
01.48.42.48.30
MÉTRO: VAUGIRARD
NOON-3PM & 7PM-11PM
CLOSED SUNDAY & MONDAY

✦

SMALL SIGNS STILL ADVERTISE COGNACS, CHAMPAGNES, CAFÉS, THÉS, CONFISERIE, the wares that once were sold here when this was a small turn-of-the-century *épicerie* in the quiet, residential fifteenth *arrondissement*. Today, the intact premises are home to a quaint corner *bistro* with a quaint play-on-words name, *"je t'aime"* (I love you).

The old grocery shelves now display the owners' growing collection of vintage kitchen canister sets, colorful majolica pitchers, brass scales, coffee grinders, and teapots; on the marble counters, bottles of wine and the restaurant's glassware are kept for the dozen or so tables in the charming, low-key dining room. Because of a strong word-of-mouth following, the establishment is often full despite an out-of-the-way location that attracts few foreign tourists. All visitors, however, receive a warm welcome from Madame, the hostess, and from Monsieur, the chef, when he emerges from the kitchen. The menu, listed on a slate chalkboard that is brought to the tables, includes an onion *terrine* served with a honey sauce, salad garnished with smoked pork, beef *carpaccio*, tuna *tartare*, duck with mushrooms, *rougets* (red mullets) roasted with thyme, crayfish *fricassée*, and roast pork. Desserts such as a fresh fruit salad, *fromage blanc* sweetened with honey, and fruit *clafoutis* complete the meal.

Saturday afternoons, Je Thé…me draws a small crowd of neighborhood residents for a homey tea service with freshly baked tarts, cakes, and pastries.

SIXTEENTH ARRONDISSEMENT

✦

Chalet des Îles

LAC INFÉRIEUR
BOIS DE BOULOGNE (16TH ARR.)
01.42.88.04.69
MÉTRO: RUE DE LA POMPE
SERVICE UNTIL 9:45PM
CLOSED DECEMBER 1-FEBRUARY 28

✦

EVEN AMONG THE SELECT GROUP OF RES-
TAURANTS LOCATED WITHIN THE LARGE
wooded parks of Paris, the Chalet des Iles, which
has been located since 1894 on one of the long, thin
islands in the largest lake of the Bois de Boulogne, is
unique. Surrounded by trees and water, the feeling
of being at a small country inn just minutes from
the center of the city is remarkable, especially given
that the Chalet's "natural" setting is the product of
complete artifice.

As Napoleon III's engineers constructed the 2,500
acres of the *bois* in the 1850s, the soil was found to
be too porous to accommodate the planned lake on
which the restaurant sits. An excavated pit was
therefore completely encased in concrete and filled
with water from artesian wells that travelled to the
site through some sixty kilometers of underground

pipe. The picturesque result, however, has been a success with generations of Parisians from Emile Zola and Marcel Proust, who were among the restaurant's early regulars, until today.

As nineteenth-century visitors did, modern diners arrive on the island by either rowboats that can be rented by the hour or by a pay ferry service. Seated beneath large umbrellas, they take in the exceptional view along with the *foie gras*, steak with *roquefort* sauce, and the duck *confit*. The restaurant is obviously a favorite destination for families, who undoubtedly also appreciate the *prix-fixe* menu for children, a rarity in Paris.

La Grande Cascade

ALLÉE DE LONGCHAMP
BOIS DE BOULOGNE (16TH ARR.)
01.45.27.33.51
MÉTRO: AV. HENRI-MARTIN
NOON-2:30PM & 7:30PM-10:30PM

✦

THE GRANDE CASCADE IS NAMED FOR THE LARGE, CRAGGY WATERFALL IT FACES IN the Bois de Boulogne, a feature of the sylvan landscape, like so much of the mid-nineteenth-century park, that is entirely manmade. Few of the fashionable Second Empire Parisians who each afternoon promenaded to the falls—the ultimate see-and-be-seen destination—were aware that this dramatic effect required enormous quantities of water that were collected in a reservoir and then released all at once for their enjoyment.

The restaurant, located near the Longchamp racetrack where Édouard Manet and Edgar Degas painted so often, continues to attract a well-heeled crowd to its outdoor terrace and formal sky-lit dining room, once the hunting lodge of Emperor Napoleon III. Large chandeliers, heavy drapes, velvet upholstery, and potted palms provide the backdrop for a cuisine that is in part classic, part contemporary: *confit* of duck *foie gras*, *langoustines* with zucchini flowers and fennel tempura, *calamari* aspic with fennel and sweet pimento, stewed chicken breast with truffle juice, caramelized duckling with spices, *fricassée* of sweetbreads and wild *escargots*, *crème brûlée* with pistachios and cherries, cold strawberry soufflé with rhubarb, and the *grand dessert* that combines hot and cold chocolate preparations.

La Grande Cascade offers a popular late-afternoon tea service daily.

ROUTE DE SURESNES
BOIS DE BOULOGNE (16TH ARR.)
01.44.14.41.14
MÉTRO: PORTE DAUPHINE
NOON-2:30PM & 7PM-10:30PM
CLOSED SUNDAY DINNER & MONDAY

✦

WHEN GASTON LACHAILLE, THE DEBONAIR HERO OF COLETTE'S "GIGI," WISHED TO give a suitably chic private supper party, he selected the Pré Catalan located in the Bois de Boulogne, one of the most stylish dining spots in Belle Epoque Paris. The elegant white pavillon in its tranquil wooded setting is still home to an exclusive, formal restaurant, although the quaint half-timbered cottage alongside the premises no longer contains the dairy where riders returning from the park's bridle paths could stop for freshly drawn milk.

Today's diners are far more likely to be sipping vintage champagne than milk as they consider a menu that features *hors d'oeuvres* such as sardine salad, chilled shrimp with *vinaigrette*, duck *foie gras*, *escargots*, roast asparagus with tomato *confit* and black olives, and main courses that might include *cabillaud* (cod) *meunière* with eggplant, turbot steamed in fresh seaweed, sole, lobster, *tournedos*, roast hare, and roast lamb shoulder.

In cold weather, a monumental fireplace more than makes up for the loss of the Pré Catalan's peerless garden terrace.

ARRONDISSEMENT

✦

Aristide

121, RUE DE ROME (17TH ARR.)
01.47.63.17.83
MÉTRO: ROME
NOON-2PM & 7:30PM-10:30PM
CLOSED SATURDAY & SUNDAY

✦

IN ÉDOUARD MANET'S FAMOUS PAINTING "LA GARE SAINT-LAZARE," A LITTLE GIRL dreamily watches trains entering and leaving the station. Manet, who had long lived in this district, painted the scene from a garden on the rue de Rome that overlooked the tracks. Then, as now, the quarter was quiet, rather featureless, and primarily residential, its inhabitants served by classic, unpretentious neighborhood *bistros* such as Aristide, which has faced this same railway cut since it opened in 1893.

Beneath a green-canvas awning, the restaurant's windows are simply decorated with lace café curtains and vintage soda siphons. The top of the menu proudly announces Aristide's old-time culinary standards: dishes are prepared with only the freshest ingredients that will be cooked in either butter or goose fat. First courses include marinated anchovies, rabbit *terrine*, lentil salad with bacon, chilled arti-

choke hearts, or *roquefort* soufflé; main dishes—
principally from the southwest of France—include
grilled *entrecôte*, *andouillette* (chitterlings sausage),
roast lamb, and, among the half-dozen preparations
of sole, grilled, *meunière*, or with sorrel sauce. For
dessert, Aristide specializes in *sorbets* and ice creams,
but also offers *clafoutis*, *millefeuille*, and plums soaked
in wine from the Cahors region.

Le Bistrot d'à Côté

10, RUE GUSTAVE-FLAUBERT (17TH ARR.)
01.42.67.05.81
MÉTRO: TERNES
12:30PM-2PM & 7:30PM-11PM DAILY

✦

NOT FAR FROM THE ARISTOCRATIC PARC MONCEAU IS A SMALL OLD-FASHIONED *épicerie*, similar to countless others that once existed in the pre-supermarket city, closed up in the mid 1980s. After providing everyday essentials to the inhabitants of the stately seventeenth *arrondissement* for nearly a century, the grocery escaped having its lovely interior completely gutted, the usual fate of most defunct businesses. Instead, noted chef Michel Rostang seized on the premises—vintage fixtures and all—as the ideal site for an unpretentious *bistro* that he would operate next door (*d' à coté*) to his more elegant eponymous restaurant.

Even the enameled letters that once advertised *Beurre Oeufs Fromages* have been preserved on the plate glass windows, beside which caned *bistro* chairs and tables now form a small sidewalk terrace. Inside, an assortment of scores of fanciful vintage majolica pitchers, vases, and pots adorn the old grocery shelves. Although the menu, posted on small slate chalkboards, changes daily according to what is freshest in the market, sample offerings include: *vinaigrette* of warm lobster raviolis, artichoke salad, asparagus risotto, *terrine* of chicken livers with pistachios, *escargots*, roast Bresse chicken, and *tête-de-veau*. For dessert, there are roasted peaches with ice cream, apples caramelized in cider with gingerbread, among other choices.

Cave Pétrissans

---

30 BIS, AVENUE NIEL (17TH ARR.)
01.42.27.52.03
MÉTRO: TERNES
WINE BAR: NOON-2:30PM & 8PM-10:30PM
CLOSED SATURDAY & SUNDAY
SHOP: 9AM-8:30PM
CLOSED SATURDAY AFTERNOON & SUNDAY

✦

EVEN IN A CITY WHERE MANY BUSINESSES HAVE OPERATED CONTINUOUSLY ON THE same site for a century or more, establishments such as Pétrissans, which is still owned by the family that founded it in 1895, are a rarity. For four generations this evolving wine business has been a neighborhood institution in the tony seventeenth *arrondissement* not far from the Arc de Triomphe.

A large sign in the shape of a wooden bottle stands at the corner entrance to the oldest part of the business, the minuscule retail wine shop, with its Art Nouveau light fixtures, elaborately patterned tile floor, and carefully selected stock displayed on the original wooden shelves. The family eventually expanded the enterprise to include a small wine bar in an adjoining room (reached through a separate street entrance) that is among the most acclaimed in Paris. Simply and comfortably furnished, the dining room includes a four-stool bar, oak tables, and banquettes upholstered in the traditional moleskin. Out on the avenue, a sizable terrace is shielded from the sidewalk by tall trellised planters.

Although the constantly changing wine list is the obvious draw here, the loyal customers also come to Pétrissans for well-prepared *bistro* standards such as *escargots*, parsleyed ham, steak *tartare*, lamb stew, chicken in a tarragon cream sauce, grilled *andouillette* (chitterlings sausage), *tête-de-veau*, and a fish of the day; desserts make use of fresh fruit according to the season in various tarts and *sorbets* or, perhaps, plums in one of the shop's best Armagnacs.

ARRONDISSEMENT

✦

Lux-Bar

12, RUE LEPIC (18TH ARR.)
01.46.06.05.15
MÉTRO: BLANCHE
7AM–11PM DAILY

✦

THE RUE LEPIC, WHICH RISES UP THE MONTMARTRE HILL FROM THE BUSY PLACE Blanche, remains one of the most colorful and historic old market streets in Paris. When this area was a self-contained village perched above the city, it was home to small tradesmen, farmers, and millers as well as to bohemian writers and artists drawn by the area's inexpensive garrets and the unspoiled provincial ambience. In the 1880s, Vincent van Gogh lived at 54, rue Lepic with his brother, Theo, near the Moulin de la Galette, the rustic outdoor dance hall that he, Renoir, and Toulouse-Lautrec each captured on canvas.

Even today, although it is just a short distance from the place du Tertre, the heart of tourist Montmartre at the hill's summit, the lower stretch of the rue Lepic remains the province of locals going about their business. Since shortly after the turn of the last century, Lux Bar, a simple café-*bistro*, has operated here among the bakery shops and horse butchers, serving generations of the market's merchants and shoppers.

In winter, old-fashioned braziers warm the dozen or so tables set out under a green awning on the precipitously steep triangular corner. Inside, the bar dominates the small wedge-shaped room that features a tile mural of the Moulin Rouge, the famed 1889 cabaret just around the corner on the boulevard de Clichy. A limited menu features a few hot meals, such as *gigot d'agneau aux flageolets* (roast leg of lamb with beans), sandwiches served on *pain Poilâne* (roast beef, ham, *saucisson*, *paté*, or *rillettes*), and a salad topped with warm goat cheese.

La Mère Catherine

6, PLACE DU TERTRE (18TH ARR.)
01.46.06.32.69
MÉTRO: ABBESSES
NOON-12:30AM DAILY

✦

WHEN THE PICTURESQUE VILLAGE OF MONTMARTRE WAS INCORPORATED INTO the city of Paris in the middle of the nineteenth century, La Mère Catherine, a *brasserie* on the main square, the place du Tertre, was already a landmark, having been in business since a few years after the French Revolution.

Today, a good deal of Montmartre—this restaurant included—is a paradox. For the entire twentieth century, the area's popularity has spared it from modernization, while transforming it into little more than a theme-park version of its former self. The place du Tertre is crowded and commercialized, with beret-clad caricaturists filling in for Renoir, van Gogh, and Toulouse-Lautrec, all of whom lived and worked in the immediate area. Even the genuinely old and historic, such as La Mère Catherine, can seem like faux recreations. That disclaimer aside, this oldest restaurant on the *place* is a surprisingly pleasant place to have a meal.

Within the rustic interior, large crocks adorn the dark wood walls hung with framed oil paintings of the nearby cabaret Le Lapin Agile, the basilica of Sacré-Coeur, and other Montmartre landmarks. Terra cotta tiles on the floor, exposed wooden beams on the ceiling, and simple wooden chairs at tables draped in homey red-and-white checked linens complete the look. Several varieties of fresh oysters are offered, as well as asparagus soup, onion tart, *pintade* (guinea fowl), *lotte* (monkfish) *provençale*, *escargots*, *marmite du pêcheur* (fish casserole), and *pot-au-feu*. *Crêpes Suzette* are among the desserts.

Special Listings

LUXURY RESTAURANTS

✦

TEA SALONS

✦

PÂTISSERIES/BOULANGERIES

✦

AUTHOR'S FAVORITES

✦

Index

CITY SECRETS ROME
edited by Robert Kahn

Tour Rome in the company of its most passionate admirers as the world's foremost artists, writers, architects, archaeologists and historians reveal their favorite discoveries in this ultimate insider's guide: a renowned painter shows the way to a hidden garden, a poet laureate shares the address of a little-known trattoria, a classicist suggests an ecclesiastical shopping spree. Detailed maps. *"...the best literary gift to Italian travelers since the Baedeker and Henry James."*–Financial Times CLOTHBOUND $19.95 ISBN 1-892145-04-9 Upcoming volumes in the City Secrets series: *City Secrets London* (September, 2001); *City Secrets New York* (September, 2001)

CITY SECRETS FLORENCE, VENICE & THE TOWNS OF ITALY
edited by Robert Kahn

If a standard guidebook has never given you entrée to the Italy you seek, let City Secrets unlock the door. Second in the acclaimed City Secrets series, *City Secrets Florence, Venice, & the Towns of Italy* brings together the recommendations of the people who know Italy best. Whether writing about a painting, a restaurant, or a village's hidden byways, the impassioned descriptions and informed perspectives in these pages, taken together, form an exhilarating tour of this most inspiring of countries. CLOTHBOUND $19.95 ISBN 1-892145-01-4

ARTISTS IN RESIDENCE
by Dana Micucci with photographs by Marina Faust

Open to the public, the homes and studios of eight celebrated 19th-century painters—Vincent van Gogh, Claude Monet, Gustave Courbet, Eugène Delacroix, Gustave Moreau, Rosa Bonheur, Jean-François Millet, and Charles-François Daubigny—provide intimate insights into their work and personalities as well as pleasurable day-long itineraries in and around Paris. Sumptuous portraits of these painters' lives and times are supplemented by detailed travel information. PAPERBACK IN SLIPCASE $19.95 April 2001 ISBN 1-892145-00-6

HARPO SPEAKS...ABOUT NEW YORK
by Harpo Marx with Rowland Barber
introduction by E. L. Doctorow

One hundred years ago, little Adolph "Harpo" Marx was literally tossed out the window of Miss Flatto's second grade classroom and onto a life on the streets. His unceremonious exit from the New York City public school system set in motion a chain of events which he describes with a mixture of sweetness and hilarity in this memoir of a child's life in an immigrant family at the turn of the century. *"...This enchanting memoir will make you regret every day you ever wasted going to school."*—John Guare HARDCOVER $16.95 May 2001 ISBN 1-892145-06-5

THE IMPRESSIONISTS' PARIS
by Ellen Williams
Walking tours of the artists' studios, homes, and the sites they painted

This guidebook pairs some of the most beloved masterpieces of Impressionism with the exact locations where they were painted. Itineraries include the artists' studios, apartments, and grave sites. Listings for restaurants, many dating from the Impressionist era, round out the tours. *"This pocketable hardcover book is a small marvel. It is fun to look at and fun to read."*—John Russell, The New York Times HARDCOVER $19.95 ISBN 0-9641262-2-2

PICASSO'S PARIS
by Ellen Williams
Walking tours of the artist's life in the city

A century after his arrival there as an unknown Spanish teenager, Paris still bears the mark of Pablo Picasso's enduring presence. Four walking tours follow the painter from the gaslit garrets of fin-de-siècle Paris to the Left Bank quarter where he sat out the Nazi Occupation. Dining recommendations include many of Picasso's favorite haunts; with full-color reproductions of Picasso's paintings,

archival photos, vintage postcards, and maps. HARDCOVER $19.95
ISBN 0-9641262-7-3

HERE IS NEW YORK
by E. B. White with a new introduction by Roger Angell

In the summer of 1949, E.B. White checked into The Algonquin Hotel for the weekend and, sweltering in the heat, wrote the remarkable *Here is New York*. The New York Times has chosen it as one of the ten best books ever written about Manhattan. The New Yorker calls it "the wittiest essay, and one of the most perceptive, ever done on the city." Based partly on his memories of Manhattan when he first came to the city as a young writer, this legendary work by one of America's literary masters is now back in print with a new introduction by Roger Angell. *"...Just to dip into this miraculous essay—to experience the wonderful lightness and momentum of its prose, its supremely casual air and surprisingly tight knit—is to find oneself going ahead and rereading it all. White's homage feels as fresh now as fifty years ago."*—John Updike HARDCOVER $16.95 ISBN 1-892145-02-2

THE CHILDREN'S TRAVEL JOURNAL
by Ann Banks with illustrations by Adrienne Hartman

Your favorite little globetrotter will create a masterpiece of memories with *The Children's Travel Journal*. While on the road, this unique diary is a fun-filled work-in-progress. Once complete, it becomes a treasured keepsake that vividly preserves memories of a special trip. Topics include: Making Plans • The Destination • First Impressions • People • Food • Landmarks & Monuments • Museums • Best Day / Worst Day • I'll Never Forget. *"...Pure fun while skillfully directing a child's observations and encouraging creativity"*—Gourmet HARDCOVER $19.95 ISBN 0-9641262-0-6

✦

THE LITTLE BOOKROOM
5 SAINT LUKE'S PLACE NEW YORK NY 10014
PHONE 212 691 3321 FAX 212 691 2011
BOOK-ROOM@RCN.COM
Distributed by Publishers Group West

NOTES

NOTES

NOTES

NOTES

NOTES

ELLEN WILLIAMS, the author of the award-winning *The Impressionists' Paris* and *Picasso's Paris*, is the former art editor of Vogue and executive editor of The Journal of Art. She edited Alexander Liberman's *The Artist In his Studio* and *Keith Haring Journals*. She travels to France several times a year and has written about Paris for Travel & Leisure, International Design Magazine, France Today, and other publications. She lives in New York City with her daughter.